The New Master Course In Hypnotism

by Harry Arons

This book is dedicated to the real pioneers
In the field of hypnotism,
THE LAYMEN
who labored long and hard, braving age-old
prejudices, to gain acceptance of hypnosis
by the public and the medical and dental
professions.., and who now face
an uncertain future.

FOREWORD BY PUBLISHER

This commemorative edition of a Hypno-Classic™ was reprinted by Advanced Studies Consultants to honor Harry Arons, a man who gave a great deal to the profession during his lifetime.

Arons died on September 9, 1997, in South Orange, New Jersey. His wife, Ethel, predeceased him on March 1, 1997. He spent his lifetime as a hypnotist but is also remembered as the founder of the New Jersey Association for Retarded Children, which was the forerunner of a national organization.

Harry Arons had a long and distinguished career in the field of hypnotism. In the early thirties he performed as a stage hypnotist throughout the New Jersey/New York area and spent several seasons entertaining in Atlantic City and Asbury Park as well as on the summer resort hotel circuit.

The Master Course in Hypnotism was used as Arons' textbook for his course in scientific hypnotism. The course was taught all over the country to professionals and laymen alike. These classes led to his establishment of the Ethical Hypnosis Training Center in New Jersey.

In 1949-50 Arons became acquainted with Dr. Rexford L. North, who also had originally come from New Jersey and who was director of the Hypnotism Center in Boston, Massachusetts. Since both men had similar facilities and business activities, they had a mutual interest, and in 1951 Harry shared his hypnosis mailing list with Dr. North, who was about to launch the *Journal of Hypnotism* for the newly formed National Guild of Hypnotists. This affiliation continued from May 1951 through February 1953, when Arons' energies were turned to a new organization that was being formed.

In 1954 Arons formed the Association for the Advancement of Ethical Hypnosis, with a group of twenty or so health professionals, most of whom had been his hypnosis students. Initially the members were physicians, psychologists, dentists, lawyers, ministers, etc., but later the AAEH admitted qualified lay hypnotists, who were called "hypno-technicians," and who were allowed to use hypnosis for therapeutic purposes only with a physician's referral or under medical supervision.

With the advent and subsequent growth of the AAEH, Arons also served as editor of *Hypnosis Magazine* and *Hypnosis quarterly* as he continued teaching and writing. In 1959, Arons widened his teaching to law enforcement personnel and in 1967 his textbook, *Hypnosis in Criminal Investigation*, was published. He is generally credited with being the first hypnotist to formally write about and teach what we know as forensic hypnosis.

The instruction in this text was transcribed directly from tape recordings of his seminars. Thus, the induction techniques and important related material are faithfully reproduced in complete, word-for-word, step-by-step detail—exactly as used in his hypnosis seminars.

The publisher wishes to acknowledge the many hours of work by John C. Hughes, DC,

BCH in preparing this classic text for 21st century publication. Dr. Hughes is a noted author and trainer, who has conducted hypnotism seminars and workshops worldwide for over 50 years. He is the recipient of numerous professional awards, including the highly acclaimed Dr. Rexford L. North award, and was a founding member of the National Guild of Hypnotists in 1950-51.

Dr. Hughes is Research Editor of *The Journal of Hypnotism* and the *Hypno-Gram*. He was consultant on hypnotism to Groliers *New Book of Knowledge*, and other leading publications. He is also the author of *Hypnosis: The Induction of Conviction*; *Auto-Suggestion*; *The Roots of Hypnotism in America*; co-author with Andrew E. Rothovius of *The World's Greatest Hypnotists*; and co-author with Dr. Dwight F. Damon of *Power Hypnosis*.

Other Hypno-Classic titles are available from:
The National Guild of Hypnotists, Inc.
PO Box 308
Merrimack, NH 03054-0308
(603) 429-9438 Fax: (603) 424-8066
NGH Email: ngh@ngh.net
NGH Web Page: http://www.ngh.net

PREFACE

I started teaching hypnosis in 1934 on a small scale; my first class was a mixed group of professional people. During the three years prior to that I had obtained my own training in hypnosis, mainly via the meager supply of available books on the subject, since schools of instruction were unknown at that time. Indeed, I had heard of only four professional hypnotists active in this country during this period, three of them stage hypnotists and one a "doctor" practicing hypnotherapy who was later exposed as a fraud. I was not aware of any physicians, dentists or psychologists openly employing hypnosis at that time, though it is probable that some unobtrusive application of hypnosis by professional (medical) operators was in progress.

In 1941 1 published a 64-page booklet called *Master Course in Hypnotism*. It was intended mainly for use as a syllabus of my course. However, on the urging of some of my students, I revised the booklet in 1948, and made it available to public through normal distribution channels. It underwent other revision in 1955 and became the main text book that I included with my courses. Early in 1960 I took it off the market completely, pending the extensive revision that was badly needed and long overdue.

In more than a quarter of a century of teaching, my course personal instruction was modified many times. I made a special point of familiarizing myself with other courses being offered, both to professionals and to laymen; I took special note the inadequacies of these courses as well as of their good points. I incorporated the important material and eliminated discussions of theory and other unnecessary verbiage. Gradually, my course developed into a thoroughly organized and complete course in scientific ethical hypnosis. Its superiority to other courses has been attested to by professional and lay students who have taken the best of the others and who are therefore deemed qualified to judge.

This book is my course in essence. The induction techniques and other important material have been transcribed in tape recordings of actual class sessions. Lacking only the practice sessions, the visual demonstrations on student-subjects and the question and answer periods, the *New Master Course in Hypnotism* is one of the first attempts to present a comprehensive hypnosis course in book form. In this sense, it is a "textbook of hypnotism."

Harry Arons
So. Orange, N.J.
January 1961

IV

FOREWORD

Were the reader to have the privilege of comparing the various professional courses in hypnosis being offered today with the course for which Harry Arons has become known, he would find a number of significant differences. I have found only one of these to be on the negative side— the fact that Arons does not teach medicine, dentistry or psychology.

His reason for this lack is simple: he is not a physician, nor a dentist, nor a psychologist; moreover, he assumes that his professional "pupils" are already competent in their respective fields—and he therefore devotes himself to teaching hypnosis, induction techniques and important related material.

Dr. Charles F. Mayer of Dallas. Texas, sums it up succinctly in a letter to Arons when he says: ". . . when a potential practitioner attends a seminar, he is primarily interested in learning techniques—and that is what you teach so effectively. I have attended several seminars given by other groups, but I can truly say that yours is the best and most practical course I know of today."

There are many things in this book that the reader will appreciate. Outside of a brief historical outline, all the inessentials have been left out. There is barely a mention of theories—because none of them answers the question "What is hypnosis?" For controversial aspects, the reader is referred to the more academic works on the subject.

On the plus side, the most outstanding thing about this book is the crystal-clear exposition of the induction techniques. Arons' "3-step procedure" forms an excellent foundation for the performance of the induction technique of one's choice in a logical manner, thus avoiding the subject's adverse reactions to ridiculous induction affirmations. For the standard methods, he selects the three he considers best in this category; his presentation of the advanced techniques, the permissive methods, the indirect (disguised) procedures with the appropriate variations that arise, leaves nothing to be desired. Each method is presented exactly as I saw it demonstrated in class, with the word-for-word, step-by-step detail that is so helpful to the student. I consider Arons' course the most methodical and thoroughly organized course available today.

This book is the main text of the Scientific Medical Hypnosis Seminars, which I direct. I am quite content to let Arons teach the techniques. This permits me to devote my energies more exclusively to the applications of hypnosis in medical and dental practice, and to the demonstrations of rapid induction, which I consider so essential to making hypnosis a practical modality in the healing arts.

Maurice E. Bryant, M.D.
Clinical Associate in General Practice
School of Medicine, University of Washington
Director, Scientific Medical Hypnosis Seminars

Lawyers and judges deal daily with the psychology of human behavior. Should it be a matter of interrogation, then those of the legal fraternity should interest themselves in the

V

subject of hypnotism. In the modern day, when the ancient concept of immediate bodily punishment and deprivation of free association with others is tempered with the endeavor to first ascertain, if possible, the causative mental factors which may have led to the overt physical act, it is well-nigh imperative that law-enforcement officials, attorneys and judges possess some degree of understanding of the human tendency to suggestive response. And this understanding, to be of value, must not be confined to theory alone, but must embrace a practical knowledge of complete hypnotic methodology and correct suggestive techniques. My acquirement of the fair degree of that knowledge and understanding, under the tutelage of the author of this work, furnishes the justification for this foreword.

Forty years in the realm of the law has impressed upon me the virtue of brevity. Brevity, as the word is here employed, signifies the ability to state or demonstrate the subject matter in a concise and succinct manner without loss of the essentials. Consequently, it is natural for me, in perusing a publication, to seek brevity without loss of essentials.

I have found that quality in this volume. In this treatise, the author, Harry Arons, has very thoroughly and effectively eliminated all padding and irrelevant matter, while, at the same time, preserving all the requisites for a complete mastery of the art of scientific hypnosis. In days gone by the mention of the word "hypnotism" immediately conjured up thoughts and associations of the occult and quackery. Today we know that hypnotism is a definitely established scientific topic with no residence in the realm of mysticism. The approach and presentation of the subject in the present work is definite and scientific.

Hypnotism—that is, the art of practical hypnotism—partakes of scientific rules and formulae, but hypnosis—that is, the mental condition of the individual—is a thing natural to all normal persons, regardless of intellectual attainments or field of endeavor. It is as natural as the mind itself. Suggestibility is a normal characteristic of the mind. All about us, in everyday life, the principles of hypnotism are evident, though for the most part, unnoticed. Our very surroundings, conversations, and activities constantly offer hypnotic suggestion. Frequently we hear of the "road hypnosis" of the driver. The daily sustained and repeated advertising on radio and TV subjects listeners to many forms of hypnotic suggestions, which are often acted upon with no conscious realization by the listener. While not universally adopted, the fact of hypnosis is increasingly being employed in our schools to the end of molding and formulating human personalities and instilling individual confidence. Thus, it seems wholly unrealistic to say that hypnosis should be confined to the healing arts. The very nature of hypnosis, the fact that it is a neural phenomenon which may be induced in natural and imperceptible ways, and the fact of the limitless phases of its beneficial effects, renders ludicrous the thought that it is subject to captivity by special interests or for a special purpose. A knowledge of hypnotism and self-hypnosis and how to use and apply it and, if need be, guard against it, is therefore even more important to the layman than to the professional.

Here, in the pages of this book, will be found a practical "college education" in the art of scientific hypnotism. The curriculum is complete and thorough in every requisite detail. The author, instructor sets forth what he has learned through a lifetime devotion to the hypnotic skills and many years of rich and varied practical and theoretical experience in the art of hypnotism, self-hypnosis, and hypnotic procedures. He emphasis the actual techniques of inducing the hypnotic state. The majority of the many volumes on hypnosis give little in the way of precise methodology, devoting only a few paragraphs to actual technique. The student of such books is understandably left in a bewildered state. He is sure to lose the essential factor of prestige because of his hesitancy and uncertainty, brought about by a lack of full knowledge of the correct inductive procedure. The volume you have before you contains full, detailed, and complete techniques, with the actual wording successfully used by the author himself. For the first time, to my knowledge, a book presents the three important steps requisite for sound, scientific, hypnotic induction. The reader will also find herein many other innovations in inductive procedures and methods, waking hypnosis, speed hypnosis, and allied phases.

The "credits" which are possible from a study of this admirable work depend entirely upon the attitude, the desire, the sincerity, the zeal, the honesty, and the persistence of the student. The success of any given technique depends largely upon the basic ability of the hypnotist to speak and act in the most effective manner at the most effective time.

Even if the student or investigator lacks any desire for actual, practical application of the extensive induction procedures herein found, a deep enjoyment and great personal assurance will be the reward supplied by the knowledge derived from the reading and study of this instructive and intensely interesting master work.

Dewey Kelley, Judge, Indiana Appellate Court

This is outstandingly the clearest, soundest, and most practical book that I have seen on how to hypnotize. It is written in a straightforward, readily understandable style. It uses admirable teaching techniques. It is remarkably free from the irrelevant, superficial and dubious material which so often pads out books on this subject.

It has been my privilege to collaborate with Harry Arons in several seminars in which the materials in this book were used, I can testify to the extraordinary effectiveness of these techniques, to the enthusiasm which their demonstration aroused in the participants in the seminar, and to the great practical value of the methods of autohypnosis which Mr. Arons has developed.

Hornell Hart, Ph.D.

Professor Emeritus of Sociology; Duke University;
Author of *Autoconditioning: The New Way to a Successful Life*

THIS IS NOT AN APOLOGY ...

This book is not intended to be a literary masterpiece—and this note is not an apology for its literary imperfections.

The New Master Course in Hypnotism is intended to impart hypnotic techniques in as effective a manner as possible. Judging from the way the author's personal instruction has been received, it has been considered advisable to transfer his oral instructions to the printed page with a minimum of editing. The major portion of the instruction material has therefore been transcribed directly from tape recordings made at several of his seminars all over the country. These parts of the book "sound like Harry Arons talking," in the words of one reviewer. This kind of "talking" may detract from proper literary construction. It is our hope, however, that the advantages of "listening to Harry Arons talking" before his classes will outweigh the literary defects of the book.

INTRODUCTION

To my knowledge, *The Master Course in Hypnotism* is the first organized textbook on the subject. It differs from others in that it contains detailed instruction for inducing hypnosis as well as a large number of methods. The course in its present form includes the best methods of the old masters, the results of the investigations of prominent European and American psychologists, the fruits of the author's own active practice and experimentation and a number of important advances in method-ology made in the past two decades. It is the main text of the course in scientific hypnosis of the ethical hypnosis training center.

This course differs in another respect. It is scientific and strictly true to fact. Hypnotism is presented stripped of its heritage of hokum and mysticism. Such things as animal magnetism, magnetic healing, and similar bugaboos are pointedly ignored. Most statements made represent a consensus. In those cases where the author's opinion is given, this fact is clearly stated. The methods explained have been tried and proven and sensationalism and exaggeration have been studiously avoided. Hypnotism is presented truly as a science. The wheat, in short, is here separated from the chaff.

This course is for beginners as well as for advanced students. To the beginners, especially, the author desires to address a few pertinent remarks. It is easy to learn to hypnotize, but only by dint of persistent practice and application may one become an expert hypnotist. The author suggests that these lessons be studied—not just read—in the order and sequence in which they appear. The preliminary tests, which form a practical screening procedure, should be thoroughly mastered. The psychology of suggestion must be well understood. The student should, in particular, be quite familiar with the attendant conditions and possible dangers and have at his fingertips the means for meeting any emergencies which might arise. The course should be completed and begun a second time before any attempts at actual induction are made. Perseverance and assiduous practice will do the rest. The author earnestly hopes that once the student has mastered the hypnotic art, he will be conscientious about its application and refrain from using it for the furtherance of questionable ends. Finally, hypnosis should be used for therapeutic purposes only by those who are qualified to do so by virtue of formal training in the healing arts, or under the supervision or direction of licensed physicians and dentists.

HISTORICAL OUTLINE

Modern hypnotism begins with Franz Anton Mesmer (1734-1815). It was he who expounded the principles of animal magnetism, a system of healing based on the belief that a disturbance of equilibrium of a "universal fluid" causes disease in human beings, and that a magnetic readjustment of this "all-pervading invisible fluid" serves to cure diseases. Although Mesmer produced the hypnotic state innumerable times, he was quite unaware of the fact; it remained for his pupil, the Marquis Armand de Puységur, to actually discover the hypnotic trance, which he called "artificial somnambulism" by analogy with spontaneous somnambulism as occurring during natural sleep.

The followers of Mesmer and Puységur adhered to the erroneous principles of animal magnetism for a long time. But in 1841, Dr. James Braid, a Manchester (England) physician, coined the word "hypnosis" from the Greek "hypnos," meaning "sleep," and the scientific era began. He put no stock in magnetism, believing rather in "fascination" (fixation) and verbal suggestion. Braid, Elliotson and Esdaile also instituted the use of hypnosis as anesthesia for both minor and major operations.

In the 1870s the famous dispute broke out between the two rival schools of thought in France, the Salpétriére or Paris School, headed by Dr. Jean Charcot, and the Nancy School, led by Professor Hypolyte Bernheim of the University of Nancy. Dr. Charcot believed "major hypnotism," as he called it, to comprise three well-defined stages, which could be produced only by physical or neurological stimulation. Professor Bernheim and his followers claimed that hypnosis was caused by, and consisted of, pure suggestion, thus making their interpretation somewhat too broad. Eventually Charcot's claims were proven to be based on false theories, and, strangely enough, indirect, inadvertent suggestion.

With suggestion firmly established, it but remained for Myers to introduce the hypothesis of the "subliminal self"—a sort of dual personality dwelling beneath the threshold of consciousness. This hypothesis was clarified and improved by several American psychologists, including Professor William James and Dr. Boris Sidis, and became known as the theory of the "subconscious mind." Its adherents are spoken of as following the New Nancy School. Such famous men as Charles Richer, Pierre Janet, Emile Coué, Paul Dubois, Ochrowicz, Mobius, Myers, Gurney, Stanley Hall, and Forel belonged to this school.

Although American hypnotists today do not generally class themselves in any of these schools, they are with very few exceptions adherents to the principles of the New Nancy School.

Contents

LESSON 1
PRELIMINARY SUGGESTIBILITY TESTS

WHAT TO DO BEFORE HYPNOTIZING
One of the principal objections to the use of hypnosis, especially in the professions, is the belief that it is too time-consuming. This would be true if the operator tried to hypnotize every person who came to him. Some people can be hypnotized quickly, with some it takes a few minutes, and occasionally you find a person who is not suitable for hypnosis at all or who requires special conditions, which do riot prevail at the moment. In order to make the use of hypnosis practical, one must be able to evaluate his subjects and determine who should be hypnotized immediately and who should be left alone. For this purpose a screening procedure is absolutely necessary. The tests that follow comprise a practical screening procedure.

Three Purposes
There are three purposes of the Preliminary Suggestibility Tests:
1. The first purpose is classification. Through these tests, the operator is able to determine whether a person is good, bad, or indifferent as a subject.
2. The second purpose involves a "warm-up" or "conditioning" of the subject. Through these tests, the subject is gradually readied to go into hypnosis. He is warmed up; he is conditioned to accept the hypnotic state. If you try to hypnotize a person "cold," without taking him through any kind of a preparation period, the chances of success are greatly diminished.
3. The third purpose of the tests is possibly even more important than the first two. As you watch your subject's responses, you will get clues from his reactions as to which of the various methods of induction are more likely to be effective. No one method, no matter how skillful one may be with it, is effective with everyone. Therefore, your skill in determining which method to use will go a long way to minimize the chances of failure.

Chevreul's Pendulum
I choose Chevreul's Pendulum as the first and one of the more important of these preliminaries because I have used it with good results in still another way—to help in the student's training. Although it was designed by M. Chevreul, a Frenchman, primarily for the purpose of testing a subject's susceptibility to hypnosis, I have used it besides as an aid in increasing the student's concentration power. It can be described as follows:
A strong thread or thin cord, or better still, a thin watch or key chain, between ten and fifteen inches long, is attached at one end to a heavy ring, key, or similar object, preferably something bright and shiny. Crystal or plastic balls, with chains attached, are available from hypnotic supply houses. The other end of the cord or chain should be fastened or hung on

the eraser end of a long pencil. This is the pendulum proper. Next a heavy circle between six and eight inches in diameter is drawn on a white background (white paper, unlined, may be used, but I have found a square of white cardboard to be more practical). Inside the circle are drawn two heavy lines crossing each other at the center. We may designate the horizontal line as A-B, the vertical line as C-D, and the center as X.

This chart is placed on a chair or low table, and the person holding the pendulum stands alongside the chair, looking down at the chart. The pendulum should be held by the pointed end of the pencil, with the thumbs and fore-fingers of both hands, so that the pencil is held horizontal and the weight on the end of the cord hangs free over the center of the chart, the point X.

You must stand upright, feet together, the body relaxed as much as possible. Your elbows must not touch your sides as your hands hold the end of the pencil, while the pendulum hangs straight down over the chart.

Now fix your eyes on the point X. The ring, key, ball or whatever you are using as a pendulum should be about on a straight line between your eyes and the point X. Now if you concentrate hard on point X, keeping your eyes fixed there steadily, the pendulum will hang still over it, perhaps rotating ever so slightly. Now move your eyes to point A of the horizontal line A-B; then move your gaze across to B, then back to A, and so on, continuing to move your eyes back and forth along the line and concentrating on it as you do so. Keep this up steadily and without interruption—back and forth, back and forth—and in a short while you will find the pendulum following the line of your thoughts and your gaze, gradually swinging further and further; the harder you concentrate the more steadily the pendulum will swing back and forth along the line.

After this has proceeded for several minutes, suddenly change from line A-B to line C-D, continuing as before, but this time making your gaze travel up and down along the line C-D. In a short while the course of the pendulum's swing will gradually change, until it is again obeying your thoughts and gaze, this time swinging up and down.

Now if you will start concentrating on the circle, with your eyes going around and around the circumference, the pendulum will again change its course and follow your mind's directions, swinging in a circle or an ellipse. If you suddenly stop and concentrate anew on the point X, the pendulum will soon come to a complete halt over the center.

This may not, of course, work with you at the first trial. But keep it up for a while, resting your mind occasionally if necessary, and making certain that the cord is long enough, the pendulum object of a sufficient weight, although not so heavy as to prevent its swinging freely, and especially that you are standing properly, relaxed, not leaning against anything, your arms slightly away from your sides—and concentrating!—that is the chief requirement.

When testing a subject with Chevreul's Pendulum you follow the same general rules that I have outlined, making certain that you instruct him fully and correctly. It is best, when telling him to gaze back and forth along the line, that you help him along at first with your finger, which you hold under the pendulum and move back and forth as desired, at about one-second intervals, at the same time repeating in monotonous tones—"back and forth ... along the line" ... This should be repeated rhythmically, monotonously. The other formulae, of course, are similar: —"up and down ... along the line ... concentrate ... up and down" etc. And—"around and 'round ... just keep it up ... 'round and 'round" etc. These verbal suggestions go a long way to stimulate the pendulum's gyrations.

This exercise may be varied in a rather interesting and amusing manner, but in this you must be careful to choose the right type of subject. A person of perspicacity is likely to feel insulted, or at best consider you a simpleton, when you propose his trying the following test: Explain that your pendulum has been chemically treated, or endowed with magnetic properties, so that it reacts to sex—in fact, that it acts as a "sex indicator." State that, if held over the arm of a male it will move along the arm, back and forth; if over a female's it will go around in a circle. Demonstrate this over your own arm, indulging in a little faking, of course, and then hand it to him to try over his own arm, over yours, and over the arm of any other person who may be present.

Strangely enough, this works quite often with, as I have pointed out, the right subjects, who are usually very suggestible, gullible, and also perhaps somewhat naive—a fact that you should not admit to them!

AUTOSUGGESTION: THE BASIC PRINCIPLE

Already in this first lesson we are employing one of the fundamental psychological principles on which hypnosis is based—the principle that we call in everyday language mind over matter; in this particular case it is mind over body. But you must realize that by this we do not mean the control by the mind of one person of the body of another but rather the power of the same person's mind over his own body. In this way you can honestly explain to a prospective subject that it is not your intention to hypnotize him with Chevreul's pendulum, but rather that you are interested in testing his concentration power, the power of his mind (not yours). This attitude on your part will make him eager to do well, and success with this and other preliminary experiments will give him a feeling of importance, confidence in you, and the desire to continue with you in your experimentation.

There is nothing magical or supernatural about the pendulum's implicit obedience to the subject's thoughts. The principle involved is a natural and scientific one, called "auto-suggestion." What actually happens is this:

You, as the subject, are holding the pendulum and concentrating on, say, the horizontal line. Guided by the movements of your eyes, your thoughts go back and forth along that line while you stand relaxed and apparently motionless. But you are not really motionless. Your mind reacts on your body, on your nerves, and causes you to make slight, imperceptible movements in the appropriate directions, movements of which you are usually unaware and which are therefore unconscious. And then you are astonished when the pendulum starts to swing along with your thoughts—apparently without any help from you!

So far I have only hinted at the importance of suggestion and auto-suggestion, and that is all that I intend to do in this lesson, beyond adding that the auto-suggestion principle is the foundation of all the preliminary exercises and experiments.

In the use of Chevreul's Pendulum in your own concentration training, remember that concentration is a condition of all-absorption in a particular task. Distractions must be ignored to the point where you are completely oblivious of everything but the job in hand—in this case concentration on a line or a circle; similarly in hypnotization it helps if you become absorbed in the task of putting your subjects into hypnosis, concentrating your attention on your task and paying no heed to any distractions that might exist. Therefore you will find that a few minutes a day with Chevreul's Pendulum will increase your concentration power very noticeably, so that by the time you are ready for the methods of induction you will be able to proceed in this work without any difficulty.

3

LESSON TWO
PRELIMINARY SUGGESTIBILITY TESTS
A SCREENING PROCEDURE

TWO TYPES OF PRELIMINARY TESTS

In discussing the Preliminary Tests as well as the induction methods that will follow, I shall be referring to two types of techniques: the authoritarian types and the permissive types.

The authoritarian techniques are sometimes referred to as the "paternal techniques," pertaining to the paternal authority in the family constellation. These techniques involve a strong, commanding, dominating approach.

The permissive techniques are sometimes referred to as "maternal or mother techniques." These are soft spoken, easy going, persuasive but they minimize the authoritarian element. It is important to discover what kind of approach is more likely to work on a given subject. A person who is submissive is likely to respond better to an authoritarian approach. On the other hand, a person who is accustomed to being in a position of authority will tend to resent the authoritarian approach. For him a permissive technique is better. Naturally, knowledge of psychological types and of human nature will help the student to evaluate his subject correctly and determine what approach is likely to be more effective with him. The tests, however, will give you a good idea of the best procedure to use. Therefore, in applying the tests, we must always be watchful for clues that will help us determine the appropriate approach.

ARMS RISING AND FALLING TEST

This test is by far the best of all the preliminary suggestibility tests. It gives you a clear picture of the subject before you, providing several clues as to how he will respond to the procedure of hypnotic induction. The Arms Rising and Falling Test can be used individually or with groups of any size.

You begin by asking everyone willing to cooperate to stand up. Make certain that they have enough room in front of them so that when they stretch their arms out, they will not touch anyone. If possible, have them stand in a straight line facing you. If there are too many, they can stand up right in front of their seats, wherever they may happen to be. Proceed as follows:

"Please stand erect but relaxed, with your feet together and your arms held loosely at your sides. Now close your eyes and keep them closed until I tell you to open them. Listen easily and effortlessly to my voice.

"This test will show how well you can use your imagination. In a manner of speaking, it is a test of the power of your own mind over your own body. With your eyes closed, raise your arms forward and upward until they are at shoulder level, with the palms facing each other. Now, turn your left arm so that the palm is facing the ceiling and extend your right thumb so that it points at the ceiling.

"Now here is where your imagination comes *Imagine ... pretend ... visualize* a large book on your upturned left palm ... let us say, a dictionary. Imagine also that your right thumb is tied with a cord and that this cord extends up into the air and is attached to a balloon filled with helium gas. Use your imagination. Imagine, think, that the balloon is pulling your right arm up and the book is pushing the left arm down. Imagine your right arm is getting lighter and lighter and rising ... your left arm heavier and heavier and falling. Right arm going up—that's it—left arm going down ... that's fine! Right arm rising ... higher, higher ... left arm falling ... lower, lower. Right arm going up ... up ... up ... up ... left arm going down ... down ... down. Right arm rising; left arm falling! Right arm going up ... left arm going down. Right arm getting lighter, left arm getting heavier." Continue in this vein for several minutes, occasionally varying the technique by raising the pitch of your voice on "rising" and lowering your voice on "falling." In other words, it's not just the suggestions, but the manner in which the suggestions are given which helps the person to respond and helps to stimulate his imagination. You can use words and expressions similar to these: "Keep on thinking your right arm is rising and your left arm is falling ... right arm rising higher ... that's it ... left arm falling lower ... that's fine! Right arm still higher and higher, left arm still lower and lower," and so on.

Then, tell your subjects to open their eyes and look at their hands and watch the way they react. Some of them may show surprise at the fact that their arms have changed their positions. They may not even have been aware of the reaction that they had. These are the best subjects—those who are unconscious or unaware of the movements of their arms. The average good subject, however, will know that his arms have separated; he felt it. The reactions were involuntary nevertheless. Of course, a few will not have responded at all. These are the subjects who possibly are not suitable for hypnosis or perhaps are not suitable for this kind of a technique. This does not mean they cannot be hypnotized. You have to test them further to see if a response can be elicited.

Occasionally, a person's arms will change very rapidly with the right arm going right up and the left arm going down. This usually indicates that the person is faking, because true, authentic hypnotic reactions are slow and sluggish. If the reactions are too rapid, you have to regard them with suspicion.

Occasionally, a person will have a reverse response. That is, when his eyes open, his left arm is slightly above his right; exactly the opposite to the intention. This may indicate two things. First of all, it indicates that he is deliberately resisting. He feels a slight reaction but intentionally reverses it. But since his eyes are closed and he cannot see how his arms are responding; he tends to overcompensate his reaction, thereby causing the left arm to end up above the right. This would therefore also indicate that the person is basically suggestible but that something is causing him to resist. Often a little discussion will help to dispel whatever fears or misconceptions he may have, with the result that he may become a good subject.

This test is a permissive test. The subjects are not commanded to do anything. They are only asked to use their imagination. If they do so, the reaction follows. Therefore, they are simply *permitted* to exhibit reactions that are within themselves. No commanding or domination s involved.

It should be pointed out that the suggestions are given in a pattern or rhythm, with the same number of syllables on "rising" and the same number on "falling." For example:

"Right arm is going up ... up ... up; left arm is going down ... down ... down. Right arm rising higher and higher, left arm falling lower and lower." The pattern and the rhythm of the suggestions are helpful in lulling a person into a responsive state.

6

THE FALLING BACKWARD TEST

This test can be done individually only. Select a subject and instruct him to stand erect but relaxed, feet together, arms at sides. Take your position behind him and tell him that you are going to test him to make certain that he is relaxed by pulling him backwards. He must allow himself to fall, but assure him that you will stop him when he has fallen only a few inches. In falling backwards, his body must remain erect with feet flat on the floor, hinging only at the ankles. He must not bend at the hips or the knees, only at the ankles. Test him by pulling him gently back by the shoulders. Stop him by placing your hands on the shoulder blades before he has fallen more than a few inches. He must be assured that he will not be allowed to fall and hurt himself If he falls straight back as desired, it indicates that he is relaxed and ready for the test proper.

Instruct him to bend his head way back so that he can see the ceiling directly above him. Now tell him to close his eyes, remaining in that position. Take your own position directly behind him, keeping one foot slightly in front of the other for good balance. Place your hands on his shoulder blades and stand fairly close so that your arms are slightly bent. In this position, you can support an individual of more than twice your weight without danger of his falling. Make suggestions as follows:

"Imagine yourself standing next to a haystack with your back to it. Think that you are falling backwards. Picture yourself standing at the edge of a haystack, falling backwards. When I take my hands away, you will fall right back. Think you are falling backwards ... falling backwards ... falling backwards." Repeat these phrases four or five times, then move your hands from his shoulder blades while you are talking. If he is responsive, he will fall right back and you must immediately stop him by grasping him by the shoulders or by pushing him back at the shoulder blades. Only a few inches are necessary; do not allow him to fall back too far. If you watch closely, you may notice that when you begin to make your suggestions of falling, the subject will often lean slightly forward instead and after a while begin to sway slightly backwards. This is a natural reaction and does not necessarily mean that he is antagonistic or resisting. Occasionally a person will actually fall forward or continue swaying forward. This may indicate that he has a fear of falling or is actually resisting in some way.

That is an authoritarian test. It is very widely known and used. It is the favorite of stage hypnotists. A person who resents authority is likely to fail to respond to the Falling Backward Test.

THE COUÉ HANDS-CLASP TEST

This test, employed originally by the famous French auto-suggestionist Emile Coué, is a rather difficult one and had better not be used on any but suggestible subjects. It is in reality a very temporary and fleeting hypnotic trance, and subjects who fail it should not be considered refractory for that reason, so long as they have reacted positively to the previous tests.

In working Coué test, the subject should stand before you looking into your eyes. You instruct him to stretch out his arms in front of him and clasp his hands tightly together, fingers intertwined. Direct him as follows in a commanding fashion:

"Make your arms stiff and rigid and squeeze your hands tighter and tighter together ... tighter and tighter. At the same time concentrate on the idea that you cannot open your hands. Think that you cannot unclasp your hands. Squeeze them still tighter and tighter and think you cannot open them. When I count 'three' you will try to open your hands, but you will be unable to do so. On the count of 'three' you will try but will be powerless to open them. You cannot open them ... squeeze them tighter and tighter ... you cannot open them! Now ... one! ... two! ... three! ... you cannot open them! Try ... but you cannot! Now stop trying!"

Beware of the person who struggles very hard to unclasp his hands, gets red in the face with effort, or perhaps tries to break them apart over his knee. In cases of this sort, the chances are that he is faking.

To sum up, we can say that persons who show positive reactions to all these tests will make excellent and very easy subjects for hypnosis proper. Those who do well with the first three and fail only with the Hands-Clasp Test may also be considered quite good subjects.

PERMISSIVE HANDS-CLASP TEST

A far superior test is the Permissive Hands-Clasp Test. Often, a person who will not respond to the authoritarian test because he resents authority will respond quite readily to the Permissive Hands-Clasp Test if he is sufficiently suggestible. Tell him to raise his arms in a comfortable position, bent at the elbows, and to hold them over his lap with the fingers intertwined and the hands loosely clasped. Continue in this vein:

"As you sit there, look down at your hands as they are loosely clasped before you. Imagine that your hands are the jaws of a vise. This is the kind of an instrument where you turn a handle or screw on one side and cause the jaws to come closer and closer together. If you are unable to imagine a vise, think of the action of a vise. You know what happens when a vise is gradually closed up—the jaws come closer and closer together. If your hands are the jaws of a vise, your hands will gradually come closer together also. Now as you keep thinking of that, as you keep imagining that, you may notice certain little reactions in your hands. One of the first reactions might be a twitch of a finger, as it seems to close down against the hand. You might notice a certain amount of pulsing of the blood in your hands and fingers. This is due undoubtedly to a gradual although possibly imperceptible tension developing. Now as the inner tension gradually increases, you may begin to feel the tension, because the pulsing of the blood will increase and you may also notice a slight blanching or whitening in your fingers where they touch one another. You may also notice a slight whitening of the knuckles and, as you see your fingers gradually close down against the backs of your hands, you may also notice that your fingertips gradually become white because the pressure of your fingertips against the backs of your hands pushes the blood out of that region, causing the whiteness. As you watch, you notice how your fingers are gradually tightening up. Every once in a while there's a twitch, a little movement, and the tightness gradually increases. You can see it now. You can see the whiteness of the knuckles. You can see the whiteness of the fingers where they cross and touch one another. You can see the whiteness of the fingertips. You can feel the tension steadily increasing. Your hands are gradually getting tighter and tighter. You can see it now; you can feel it as well. Now, your hands are so tight; they're tight as a vise that has been locked. Your hands are clasped tightly together, locked like a vise, and you cannot open them! When I say 'three' you will try to open them and you will not be able to do so. One! ... your hands are getting tighter and tighter ... they're tightly clasped and you cannot open them. Two! ... they're glued together, tightly stuck and you cannot open them ... locked tightly like a vise! Three! ... you cannot open them! Try but you cannot! Now stop trying! As you relax your hands, they open up easily now. That's fine."

There is a gradual buildup in the way you make these suggestions. You start out very permissively, softly, easily, slowly. As you see the reactions that you are describing, you point them out so it seems to the subject that his reactions precede the suggestions that you made and thus you gradually lead him along. You point out each thing that you see occurring—the whiteness of the fingers, the blanching of the knuckles, the gradual closing up of the fingertips against the backs of the hands, the steadily increasing tension. As you proceed in this manner, he becomes more and more convinced that it's working because he can see it working. He gets the impression that it's working from within himself rather than because you are causing it. He is not being commanded to do anything. Towards the end of the test, of course, when you challenge him to open the hands, you become firmer and more commanding for greater emphasis and effectiveness.

It is important to be able to differentiate between the Authoritarian and the Permissive Hands-Clasp tests and to be able to judge which type is more likely to succeed on a given subject.

LAW OF WILL VERSUS IMAGINATION

It is appropriate at this time to explain briefly the law governing auto-suggestion. We can advantageously cite Coué's illustration of a wooden plank placed across the floor. You will without hesitation step onto it, walk back and forth on it, even balance yourself on one foot without the slightest danger of falling off But suppose this same board is used as a bridge between the roofs of two ten-story buildings—would you dare step onto it? And if you did, what chance would you have of maintaining your balance? Very little, you will grant, unless perhaps you were a circus performer accustomed to heights and therefore unafraid.

Much as you may desire to live, and as much WILL as you may exercise to keep your equilibrium, the fear that you will fall—imagining that you are falling—may actually make you fall. It does not matter how much WILL you use, the imagination will win. The law, therefore, is stated as follows:

"When the will and the imagination come into conflict, the imagination invariably wins."

Of course, there are people, such as circus performers, who are perfectly at ease at dizzy heights. Why? Merely because their imaginations and wills are not in conflict, but rather working in cooperation. They don't imagine themselves falling, they entertain no fear of the possibility, and therefore the all-powerful imagination, instead of working against the will, is allied with it, thus producing perfect confidence. For the same reason you are perfectly safe on the plank on the floor. It would be ridiculous for you to imagine that you are losing your balance and that you are falling to your death from a board on the floor. So here your imagination and will are in agreement, resulting in self-confidence. You should now understand why, in the preliminary tests, I so often use the words *imagine, picture, think,* etc. You should understand that imagination is the most potent factor in auto-suggestion; if you do, you will have better results with the Preliminary Tests, and later with hypnosis proper.

LESSON THREE
PRELIMINARY SUGGESTIBILITY TESTS
(Continued)

PROGRESSIVE RELAXATION TEST

The next test, if successful, actually puts a person into hypnosis, although he may not be aware of this fact.

To prepare for this test, have the subject seated comfortably or lying supine. Make sure that his back is supported and that if he is seated, his feet are flat on the floor. Do not allow him to cross his knees or even his ankles. When he is all set, tell him to close his eyes, and proceed as follows:

"The relaxation procedure is really quite a simple one, as you are about to learn. After you've closed your eyes, the first thing you want to do is make sure that your teeth and jaws are not clenched and tense—the area of the jaws and throat plays an important part in relaxing or the failure to do so. So open your mouth slightly, separate your jaws just a bit—make sure your teeth are not clenched. Fine. Now your throat muscles will have a better chance to relax.

"We will now proceed to relax every part of your body progressively. While we are doing this you will hear my voice clearly and distinctly even though it may go down to a whisper from time to time. You will be aware of your surroundings, although you may care less and less about what goes on around you.

"As you sit there quietly, direct your thoughts to the general area of your throat ... and think ... imagine ... that your throat muscles are becoming relaxed. Do this easily ... effortlessly ... that's important, as effort tends to defeat its own purpose.

"Now direct your thoughts to the top of your head ... your scalp ... and think that the tension that exists there is rapidly vanishing. Your scalp is becoming less and less taut and the top of your head is becoming completely relaxed. Now think of your forehead and your eyes and all the small muscles groups in that region and permit these muscles to become relaxed. That's it ... Just let yourself go ... and relaxation in this area will naturally follow. Now return for a moment to the throat area. You should be able to actually feel how much more relaxed this region is now than it was before we started. Relaxed ... fully and completely relaxed.

"Simply by thinking of certain parts of your body ... by dwelling on the idea of those parts becoming relaxed ... you are able to throw off all tension like a mantle and with it all fatigue and irritation. That's what relaxation can do for you. Now visualize your neck and shoulders ... and permit your neck and shoulder muscles to relax. Now think of your chest ... all the muscles and organs within your chest ... and let these relax completely. Place your attention upon the region of your diaphragm ... and relax ... relax. Your abdomen ... all the muscles and organs within that area ... allow them to become flaccid and relaxed. And now the pelvic region ... and relax, fully, completely relaxed. Think of your thighs ... and relax all your muscles there. Your knees ... the calves of your legs ... relax ... relax ... relax. Your ankles

... feet ... your very toes ... relax ... Fully relaxed. Just let yourself go completely ... just go Limp all over ... permit every organ, every fiber of your being to become completely, profoundly relaxed. It feels so restful, so pleasant, to be fully relaxed. You are now completely relaxed."

With experience, you will learn signs and indications of your progress with individual subjects. As a general rule, if the subject is restless, keeps clearing his throat or swallowing unduly, moving his hands and feet, it is not likely that he is being favorably influenced. In this case you may have to repeat the procedure, perhaps several times, before you test him for hypnosis. When he is completely immobile, you may proceed as follows:

"The condition in which you are at present is called 'progressive relaxation.' It is the Nth degree, a state of relaxation that very, very few people can attain unaided. In this condition you are so profoundly relaxed that you don't seem to care what goes on around you, although you can hear my voice very clearly and distinctly. Your arms and legs—if you'll think of them for a moment—feel rather heavy ... they are so relaxed ... and also quite numb and dull, though pleasantly so. In fact your entire body feels heavy in this condition ... heavy ... so heavy that it seems that it would require a superhuman effort to move a muscle.

"Your eyes, especially the muscles around your eyes, and your eyelids ... feel so heavy and relaxed, that it seems they are glued shut. Your eyelids are heavy as lead ... so heavy that it seems it would be impossible to raise them. The muscles controlling your eyes are so relaxed ... so flaccid and inert ... that you probably could not activate them, could not open your eyes if you tried. When I say 'three'—and not before then—I want you to try to open your eyes, but you will be amazed to find that you are completely powerless to move those muscles, quite unable to open your eyes. I'll count to 'three' and on every count your eyes will become more and more relaxed, your muscles in that area more and more flaccid and inert ... and when I reach the count of 'three' you will find that you are unable to open your eyes, powerless to raise your eyelids."

By this time you have become gradually more intense in your manner, slightly more authoritarian and direct. You speak more rapidly, so that your subject does not have time to think around your suggestions.

"Now, ONE! ... Your eyes are stuck tightly together. The muscles around your eyes are relaxed, flaccid, and limp. TWO! ... Your eyelids are heavy as lead ... stuck and you cannot open them. You are completely powerless to open your eyes ... you cannot open your eyes ... you cannot open them. THREE! ... They're stuck ... tightly stuck! You cannot open your eyes ... you cannot open them! Try ... but you cannot open them! They're stuck ... tightly stuck! Now stop trying! ... And relax completely."

Don't let him try too long; a few seconds is sufficient. Your luck must not be pushed too far. After he has stopped trying, keep talking to him for a while, urging him to go into a deeper state of progressive relaxation. You must by this time have realized that the term "progressive relaxation" is but a substitute for hypnosis and that in other respects the induction procedure is pretty much the same as the direct verbal suggestion method.

Actually, the Progressive Relaxation Test produces hypnosis, though the subject is not aware of the fact unless you explain it to him. So you see how by the gradual progression of the Preliminary Tests you bring the subject close to, if not actually into, hypnosis.

To awaken him, you simply tell him that upon the count of "five" (or any other signal) he will open his eyes and come out of the state of progressive relaxation. It's as simple as that. And your subject may never suspect for a moment that he was in hypnosis.

INDICATIONS OF THE SCREENING PROCEDURE

After having taken a subject through the foregoing tests certain indications should have developed.

If the person has responded to the Pendulum Test, the Arms Rising and Falling Test, and the Permissive Hands-Clasp Test, you can be fairly certain that he will respond well to a permissive induction method. If he has done better with the Authoritarian Hands-Clasp Test, and if he succeeded well with the Falling Backward Test, the indications are that an authoritarian approach may be preferable. If he has responded equally well to all the tests, then it actually doesn't matter what kind of approach you use. He is a "pushover" as a subject. Now the Progressive Relaxation method has both authoritarian and permissive aspects, so it cannot be properly classified. Therefore, the Progressive Relaxation Test can be used as an induction method with either kind of subject.

LESSON FOUR
RECOGNITION AND CLASSIFICATION OF SUBJECTS

QUALIFICATIONS OF A SUBJECT

Psychology will teach you that a person's traits, characteristics, temperament, intelligence, and many other factors give indications of his susceptibility to hypnosis.

Generally, it may be said that every normal person is hypnotizable. The principal exceptions are infants, the insane, and the mentally deficient. However, there are exceptions to the exceptions.

By an infant we mean a child under six or seven. It has been found, however, that a precocious child of four or five may be hypnotizable, while a child of subnormal development at the age of eight or nine may not be.

The insane cannot be hypnotized while they are actively disturbed. However, in comparatively lucid periods, they may be inducted into hypnosis quite easily.

A person with a schizophrenic trend cannot be hypnotized if he is too withdrawn. However, in the early stages, he may be quite a good subject.

Persons of the paranoid trend are most difficult to hypnotize. They are much too suspicious. Suspicion, distrust and delusions of persecution are characteristic of their disorder.

Among manic-depressives, hypnosis is possible during the manic or excitable phase but is rarely possible in the depressed phase. It is fairly certain that the feeble minded, or the mentally deficient, can't be hypnotized at all. They do not have sufficient mental development. It is fairly safe to say that a person with an IQ of 70 or less is not hypnotizable.

90% HYPNOTIZABLE

An expert hypnotist should be able to hypnotize 80% of susceptible subjects in three or four attempts. Another 10% may be inducted into hypnosis with additional attempts and different methods.

The remaining 10% cannot be hypnotized at all. There are numerous reasons, such as unconscious resistance, lack of faith in the operator, or perhaps a natural antagonism to him or his type. There are, however, instances where these conditions do not exist and yet some people simply cannot be hypnotized. Until we find out more about the nature of hypnosis, we will probably never know exactly why a small percentage remains refractory.

The above refers to expert hypnotists. However, even a beginner should be able to influence 40% or 50% of pre-tested subjects. As he gains skill, he should steadily develop to the point where he can hypnotize at least 80% of his subjects.

AGE AND SEX

A child of 7 to 8 is considered to be in the most suggestible period of life. However, suggestibility is not necessarily synonymous with hypnotizability, although it is an important ingredient. A child of 7 or 8, therefore, can appear to be easily hypnotized but when tested for depth will be in a very shallow state of hypnosis. A child that young does not seem capable of deep hypnotic trance.

From 8 to about 14, the mind rapidly develops. The period from 14 to 21 is by far the best period both for ease of induction and for depth of hypnosis. From 20 upwards, there is a gradual decline in hypnotizability. This does not mean that an 80-year-old person cannot be a good subject. It simply means that there are fewer good subjects in the older groups.

Sex seems to be a factor also. We have more female subjects than male subjects. This may be due to the fact that most operators are males. I dare say that if we had an equal proportion of male and female operators, we would probably have an equal proportion of male and female subjects. At this point, however, it seems that a male operator is more successful with a female subject and vice versa.

COMMON FALLACIES

Whether a person is brunette, blond or red haired has no bearing on his susceptibility to hypnosis. A subject does not have to be weak minded and the operator does not have to be strong willed. In fact, if we take an operator with just an average will and a subject with a strong one, and if the subject simply sets his will aside temporarily, hypnosis can result. It's more important for a subject to have a good mind than the operator, because the power or capability for hypnosis is actually in the subject.

OCCUPATION

People engaged in occupations of a monotonous or strictly routine character seem to become unusually susceptible to hypnosis. Factory workers, for example, who perform the same motion or series of motions at a machine throughout the day tend to become peculiarly susceptible. Their minds seem to get into a static mental cycle that is conducive to the induction of hypnosis.

People who are accustomed to implicit obedience are good subjects. The best example is soldiers. For this reason, we always see soldiers picked out of an audience where a stage hypnotist is performing because the hypnotist knows that these subjects are best. Soldiers become accustomed to obeying verbal commands without question. They also are obedient to symbolic commands. For example, the sight of a uniform or an insignia causes them to salute almost automatically. It's almost as if the salute had become a conditioned reflex.

Very religious people are good subjects for pretty much the same reasons. Religious people, especially those who are fanatically religious, are unquestioningly obedient to the dictates of tradition.

Leisurely workers, especially those with a scientific bent, tend to be refractory with the usual methods. Engineers, for example, and other scientific workers who require that every-thing conform to definite physical laws, who require that two and two make four, are not generally susceptible. With hypnosis, the sum of two and two is not always four. The subject has to be capable of accepting statements even though they may not be scientifically factual. However, scientists can be hypnotized by other than standard methods. People who are ac-customed to analyzing everything are, for the same reason, refractory under the usual con-ditions.

CLIMATE AND NATIONALITY

Climate and nationality seem to be factors in susceptibility to hypnosis.

People who are born and bred in the torrid zones are better subjects, probably because of their becoming accustomed to relaxing. They are conditioned to assume a state of complete lassitude, which is conducive to the attainment of hypnosis. As we go towards the colder climates, susceptibility seems to decrease.

In considering nationalities, we find substantiation for the above. We find, for example, that the French, Spanish, and the Italians are especially good subjects. These are the so-called "hot-blooded races." These people are sensitive, impressionable, expressive, emotional, passionate—all the qualifications of good subjects. Among the Germans, the English, and the Americans, we have a wide range of subjects, from the very best, to the very worst. They vary in their suggestibility according to their individual personality differences.

The inhabitants of the Indies are particularly good subjects, probably because they are so prone to believe in the mystical and the occult, as evidenced by the Voodoo rites and ceremonies and similar activities on some of the islands.

The Japanese and Chinese were not experimented with sufficiently for anything definite to be said regarding their hypnotizability, but they are probably susceptible with operators of their own race and nationality.

Persons of artistic temperament make excellent subjects. They are usually very imaginative, which is the chief requirement, and more or less sensitive. These characteristics make them very impressionable and suggestible.

People who are neurotic generally make good subjects, unless the nature of their neurosis militates against their being cooperative. If we can assume that a person with neurotic complaints has been influenced by negative suggestion, we can logically conclude from that fact that he has basic suggestibility, which has been directed in the wrong channels.

The most important personal qualifications of a good subject are imagination, sensitivity, and impressionability. If a person has these characteristics, they will usually compensate for other factors which are not favorable to the induction of hypnosis.

LESSON FIVE
FAVORABLE AND UNFAVORABLE INFLUENCES

Certain conditions of the immediate environment are conducive to the induction of hypnosis, while others prove definite hindrances. The beginner should learn these conditions thoroughly in order to avoid unnecessary failures. The expert hypnotist need not concern himself so much about favorable and unfavorable conditions because, when he occasionally fails, it does not affect him adversely. But the beginner cannot afford to be negligent in this respect. A series of failures might have a deflating influence on his ego. On the other hand, nothing succeeds like success, so it behooves the beginner to observe as many of the favorable conditions as possible in order to assure continued success.

Generally speaking, a subdued lighting effect is best for the induction of hypnosis. If it is daytime, shades should be drawn in order to produce a subdued effect. If it is at night, colors can be used to produce the most beneficial atmosphere.

It has been found that blues and greens are the best colors for the induction of hypnosis. They seem to have a restful and soothing effect. Anything in the red family seems to be irritating and tiring and should be avoided. Red, orange, and yellow, therefore, should be avoided during induction of hypnosis.

INFLUENCE OF TEMPERATURE

An even temperature, perhaps slightly on the warm side, favors bodily comfort during induction. Extremes of hot or cold should be avoided. Sudden cold drafts of air should be carefully avoided. It has been found that a sudden draft of air can hinder induction or may even completely awaken a person who has already been hypnotized. Watch for drafts from fans, open windows, and air conditioners. Once a person is in hypnosis, however, and if it happens to be a bit too warm or a bit too cool, the temperature can be modified by simple suggestion.

INFLUENCE OF ODORS

Common sense dictates that when one works in close proximity to someone else, as you do in hypnosis, one should avoid the unpleasant odors of onions, garlic, etc. However, there are some things which are not so obvious about which we should also be careful. Some subjects in hypnosis will become extremely intolerant of things which they are able to stand under normal conditions. For example, a non-smoker, who is able to tolerate the smoking of people around him, under hypnosis may find the presence of tobacco extremely irritating, to the extent that he may fail to go into hypnosis or awaken prematurely. Therefore, if you know a person does not smoke, even though he has not expressed himself to be against it, be on the safe side by avoiding smoking during the induction of hypnosis.

Actually, incense could be helpful as it could be obtained in different scents. However, the use of incense is not desirable due to its association with the mystical and the occult.

Therefore, if anyone decides to use incense, he might as well wear a turban and adopt the title of Swami.

INFLUENCE OF MUSIC AND SOUND

Music has a calming and relaxing effect on human beings as it does on animals and is therefore helpful in the process of induction of hypnosis. When music is employed, it should be used as a background. It should not be too loud and may emanate from an adjoining room or a closet. The sound should be subdued. Tape recordings and record players can be put to use for this purpose.

In addition to music, certain sounds are helpful. Any monotonous sound can be an aid. The metronome is an example. The sound of a fan motor, or the motor of an air conditioner can be helpful. Certain sounds in high and low frequency ranges are sometimes used for induction. It has been reported that experiments are being conducted with ultrasonic sound but the results of these experiments have not yet been made known.

INFLUENCE OF QUIET

The importance of perfect quiet has been greatly exaggerated. Naturally it is helpful if there are no distractions during the induction process. But the usual sounds of traffic and other activity will not hinder induction. Unless the operator sounds annoyed, for he will transfer his feelings to the subject. If the operator pays no attention to the usual sounds in the surroundings, the subject will not either. The attitude of the operator is all-important in this respect. Sometimes, sounds of traffic can be used as a helpful influence. During the induction process, a suggestion can be made that whatever sound the subject may hear from the street will have a soothing and lulling effect; thus apparent adverse circumstances can be turned to good advantage.

I made a study of this problem over a six-month period. During this period I had two offices, one completely soundproof, the other in a very noisy spot. I found no appreciable difference in the results in these two offices.

INFLUENCE OF EASE AND COMFORT

Personal comfort naturally aids the induction of hypnosis. There are a few things which we must watch.

If the subject is seated, you have to make sure that his back is supported against the back of his chair. His feet should be flat on the floor or, if a footrest is available, they must be supported on that. Knees must never be crossed and the ankles must not be crossed. His hands should rest on the arms of the chair or on his thighs or loosely on his lap. The arms must never be crossed on the subject's chest or placed on any part of his body except his thighs. The mere weight of the hands or arms on the chest or abdomen may be a hindrance. If a backrest is available for the head, this is helpful but it is by no means necessary. The head should be held in an evenly balanced position. Usually, but not always, as a person relaxes and goes into hypnosis, the head falls forward or to one side. You must be careful not to allow the head to fall back as it relaxes. Should you notice the head tilting backward, it is permissible to move it forward in order to get it started in that direction.

If the subject assumes a recumbent position his arms should lie alongside of him and his head should be slightly elevated from the body. The important thing to remember is that the subject's posture should be such as to allow complete relaxation of his entire body.

Be certain also that his clothing is loose, tie and collar open if too tight, belt eased, and shoes, if not comfortable, removed. With female subjects pay particular attention to corsets and shoes.

INFLUENCE OF PHYSICAL CONDITIONS

If a person is in pain or under any kind of physical discomfort, this is usually a hindrance to the induction of hypnosis. If he has a temperature, no matter how slight, if he is perspiring unduly, these also are hindrances. Some subjects have cold and clammy hands and feet. These conditions should be corrected before induction is begun. They should be instructed to dry their hands with a handkerchief and rub them vigorously together, meanwhile walking briskly around the room to stimulate circulation in the extremities.

Occasionally, the presence of severe pain actually becomes an incentive for a person to seek relief in hypnosis. There have been a number of cases where unbearable pain was actually used as a springboard to get a person into hypnosis. But these are exceptions, rather than the rule.

If a person is overtired, this works against hypnosis. Physical exhaustion may put a person into a natural sleep rather than into hypnosis. Actually, the closer a person's condition is to normal, the better it is for the induction of hypnosis.

If a person is intoxicated, it is a definite hindrance. Intoxication impairs his ability to concentrate. The influence of drugs is likewise unfavorable. It seems that any condition which clouds the mind or which dulls the higher centers of the brain is a hindrance to the induction of the hypnotic state. Under some conditions a minor dosage of drug can be used as a "placebo" to help induce hypnosis. In these cases, however, it is the suggestive effect that does the work, rather than the drug. In most cases drugs are hindrances. Even tranquilizers should be avoided.

INFLUENCE OF THE EMOTIONS

If the subject's emotions can be aroused in favor of being hypnotized, this facilitates matters greatly. One of the best ways of arousing a person's emotions in that way is to have him observe someone else being hypnotized. Many hypnotists set up their offices in such ways that newcomers are given the benefit of observing other subjects in hypnosis, in order to arouse their expectation of being hypnotized to the maximum. Stage hypnotists use this factor to advantage. They always pick the best subject first. Their success with the first subject in an important factor in arousing the expectation of the succeeding subjects. On the contrary, should the first attempt fail, the hypnotist may have a whole line of failures before he can break the wrong influence.

Generally speaking, love, respect, trust, prestige of the operator, are favorable influences to the induction of hypnosis, while anger, irritation, distrust, hate, are unfavorable. Occasionally, a certain type of fear of the operator can be a conducive influence. This, however, is more a fascination or awe than an actual fear.

Judging prospective subjects accurately by quickly analyzing their personal qualifications will save the hypnotist much time. Then he can further eliminate undesirable or refractory subjects by means of the preliminary susceptibility tests, thus assuring success when he finally proceeds to induce hypnosis proper.

LESSON SIX
DANGERS OF HYPNOTISM
AND HOW TO AVOID THEM

Before you attempt to actually hypnotize anybody, you must know what precautions to observe and exactly what to do should an emergency arise.

The actual dangers of hypnosis can be minimized provided the operator is thoroughly familiar with hypnotism. We might say that this is true in the sense that driving an automobile is harmless if the driver knows how, or conversely, that eating might be dangerous because a person might choke on the food he eats. You will agree that outlawing eating and driving because of these dangers would be ridiculous. On the other hand, practicing hypnotism without knowing the hazards and being familiar with the methods of meeting possible emergencies would certainly be unwise.

The first and most important danger to consider is the danger to the hypnotist. Hypnosis is an interpersonal relationship of great delicacy and like other relationships can develop disturbances and trouble.

Because of the stigma attached to hypnosis, there is always a risk that a female subject may accuse a male operator of improper conduct if in doing so she might be able to get some money out of the hypnotist. Such willful charges are comparatively rare, however. Another possibility is that a certain type of subject, usually a female, may develop an undue attachment to the hypnotist. This attach-ment, when occurring between a doctor and patient, is often referred to as "transference" and is a familiar phenomenon among physicians, dentists, and psychologists. With a certain type of female subject, generally the frustrated old maid type, there is a chance that the hypnotic relationship might cause what is known in psychological circles as "rape fantasy." This is a feeling of conviction on the part of the subject that she was actually raped by the operator. It has happened to professional people in the various specialties, particularly where a general anesthetic was involved, that such disturbed patients brought charges of improper conduct against them, to the extent that there actually have been court trials. With hypnotists the same thing may occur with the same type of subject.

The best precaution against this possibility is to have a third person present while hypnotizing females who appear disturbed. Of course, once you learn that the subject may be trusted, the precaution is no longer necessary. Ordinarily the presence of a third party will discourage unscrupulous people from attempting to take advantage of situations of this kind. The above precaution is particularly important for the lay hypnotist. While the physician and dentist are covered by malpractice insurance policies, the layman is not. Therefore, should charges be brought against him, the liability is entirely his own.

Occasionally the question arises: what would happen to a subject should the operator fall sick or for some other reason be forced to leave a subject without awakening him? there is no danger at all. The simplest thing to do is to place the hypnotized person on a bed or couch and let him "sleep it off." He will awaken of his own accord in a few minutes—never will a subject sleep without specific command for more than a half hour or so. A hypnotist who expects to be called away for any reason can, as a precaution, instruct his subject to obey the commands of an assistant he names, who will then proceed to do the awakening.

You should avoid subjecting the hypnotized person to sudden shocks. The sudden announcement of the death of a loved one, for example, or the declaration that the building is on fire, would shock him in exactly the same way as it would if he were in a waking state. Should the person be prone to heart attacks, such a shock might cause a heart attack. The fact that he's hypnotized would not obviate the possibility.

Avoid changing the subject's emotions from one extreme to another. There is a favorite hypnotic stunt in which the subject is made to see a comedy on television, causing him to laugh. Then he is told to see a tragedy and to cry. Changing the emotions too quickly, from laughing to crying, may be upsetting to a delicate nervous system. Common sense will tell you to avoid such antics.

Catalepsy should be induced gradually. For example, if catalepsy of the arm is induced suddenly, at a snap of the fingers, the sudden movement, the sudden stiffening of the arm, can conceivably strain a muscle or crack or tear something. The thing to remember is that a source of danger at any time can be a similar source of danger under hypnosis.

Some people are still laboring under the fallacious belief that hypnotic subjects can withstand the destructive influence of heat, cold, injuries and so on. This is not true. A subject may be anesthetized and told to hold his fingers in a flame without feeling the pain, but his flesh would be seared nevertheless. With his arm anesthetized he would not feel the pain of a needle under his skin, but if the needle is not sterile, infection may result. The old catalepsy test, where the body is made rigid and supported between two chairs with weights being placed on the subject's middle, is also dangerous. While a hypnotized person can support such weights, should he have an inner weakness, such as a hernia, this stunt might easily do real damage.

Common sense will tell you that if you make a subject stare wide-eyed at the sun, hypnotized or not, this could cause blindness. The person under hypnosis might be able to lift weights which he could not lift in a waking state, but unless he knows how to lift, such exercise might cause a strain. A subject might be tricked into eating ground glass and other harmful substances, believing them to be food, but it stands to reason that such activity can result in real damage. It must not be forgotten that a person, though hypnotized, is still human, and cannot do anything harmful without suffering the consequences attendant upon such actions.

THREE PRINCIPAL DANGERS

1. Cardiac Cases

A person with a bad heart should not be hypnotized except for medical purposes, and under medical supervision. I do not mean that hypnosis can be harmful in cardiac conditions. The possibility, however, that the subject might sustain a shock in hypnosis which would cause a heart attack might prove embarrassing to the operator. The same shock received under hypnosis or in the waking state might kill him, but should it unfortunately happen in the hypnotic trance, the operator would probably, though unjustly, be held accountable. Of course, when this is done under medical supervision, the physician present would know how to deal with a heart attack.

2. Hysterical Cases

People who are hysterical, who tend upon slight provocation to experience laughing, crying, or various other types of seizures, should also be avoided except for therapeutic

24

purposes. Although no actual harm can occur from hysterical seizures, a person falling into such a state can make a very unpleasant scene and can cause spectators to lose confidence in the operator and to exaggerate the dangers of hypnosis. The lowering of the threshold of consciousness causes such disturbances. That is, while undergoing induction, a subject's self-control is slackened, his conscious control is removed; whatever troublesome impulses, which have been hitherto repressed or held back are present and suddenly rise into consciousness, resulting in an outburst of hysterics.

Should this occur, the subject should on no account be immediately awakened. Awakening him during a hysterical fit would remove the possibility of hypnotic control and would leave him without any conscious control. The hysterical episode would then have to run its course; it might take as long as half an hour before it would be completely dissipated.

Instead, the operator should do his best to calm the subject, keeping him under hypnosis and talking to him in soothing tones. Thus, the duration of the seizure would be lessened, although it could not be eliminated completely by suggestion. The subject should be awakened only after he has been fully calmed and has taken hold of himself Whatever spectators are present must be kept quiet and prevented from calling the police or other authorities, whose intervention could really do nothing but aggravate the condition and possibly create panic. It is in just such emergencies that a hypnotist's personal qualities, particularly self-possession, are of the greatest advantage to him.

Fortunately, hysterical subjects can be recognized in most cases prior to induction or during the induction process. Usually, as a subject begins to go under, he betrays hysterical reactions with certain unmistakable signs. The most common sign is a back and forth movement of the head—a rhythmic, continuing movement. Sometimes the movement of the head is circular or elliptical. It is a rocking or swaying movement. Occasionally the movement is coordinated with exaggerated breathing so that a person breathes deeply and heavily in time with his rocking. Occasionally the hands and fingers tremble or the knees move back and forth in a peculiar rhythmic and continuing fashion. I am not referring here to an occasional movement, but a continuing movement in a rhythmic pattern.

These movements indicate the lowering of the threshold of consciousness and the arousal of subconscious reactions. It actually indicates that the subject is beginning to go into hypnosis. The thing to do at this point is to stop making hypnotic suggestions, or suggestions of going into hypnosis. Instead, start making suggestions of calmness, self-control, relaxation, peace, tranquility, serenity, and so on. At the same time, make soothing motions over the forehead and over the temples and under cover of these motions, take hold of the head and slow up the movements; but do it casually so that the subject does not notice that you are in any way concerned. Having physically stopped the movements and calmed him down, let go of his head, keep on talking and see whether the movements will resume. They may not. The movements might only have been indications of a tendency toward hysteria, but there might riot be an actual hysterical episode resulting. In this case, you can proceed with the induction process.

However, should the movements resume, stop them again by using the same method, calm him down completely, and when he is perfectly still, gradually bring him out of it, and leave him alone.

For therapeutic purposes, in the hands of a psychiatrist or clinical psychologist, a hysterical seizure might actually be helpful. It might be helpful in unearthing hidden causes of his trouble. It might also be helpful as a psychological cathartic, releasing from the subconscious troublesome impulses and feelings. Often, when these pent up feeling are released, a person feels much better. A layman should avoid any contact with this kind of situation.

3. *Unqualified Therapy*

One of the major dangers—not of hypnosis, but of its improper use—is the possibility that a person who needs help may go to a hypnotist who is unqualified to treat him. The delay in seeking qualified help may not only be dangerous, but conceivably actually fatal. Only physicians and clinical psychologists should use hypnosis for therapeutic purposes. A layman has no right in this area unless he is performing specific functions as prescribed by a licensed physician. A layman is not able or permitted to diagnose cases and may therefore fall into the trap of trying to treat symptoms without being aware of the cause.

There is some danger of precipitating emotional disturbances in some people. If a person is psychologically ill, he should seek proper help. Hypnotizing a person with emotional disorders might conceivably precipitate more trouble. Therefore, if a subject shows any signs of instability, the lay hypnotist should avoid working on that person unless he is instructed to do so by a licensed practitioner.

Age regression is a remarkable phenomenon but one which should be left in the hands of a qualified practitioner of the healing arts and possibly should be limited to psychiatrists and clinical psychologists. Through age regression, it is fairly easy to arouse emotional disturbances, which a person might have been holding in check. Although there have been no documented cases of psychoses precipitated by hypnosis, the possibility exists. The recommendation therefore is that age regression be used only as a therapeutic tool and only by those qualified to practice psychotherapy.

LESSON SEVEN
PSYCHOLOGY OF HYPNOTISM

What actually is hypnosis? What causes the hypnotic trance? What are its characteristics? Dr. Boris Sidis, a pupil of the great Professor William James, defines it thus: "Hypnosis is an abnormal (or super normal) state of mind, induced by artificial means, and characterized chiefly by the presence of suggestibility." If we analyze this definition closely we find suggestion to be the dominant factor: the artificial means that Sidis speaks of are suggestion; the result of these means hypnosis is a condition or mental state of increased suggestibility, a condition favorable to the acceptance of the operator's suggestions or commands. What, then, is suggestion?

Sidis says: "By suggestion is meant the intrusion into the mind of an idea; met with more or less opposition by the person (subject); accepted uncritically at last, and realized unreflectively, almost automatically."

Baldwin understands suggestion to be: "A great class of phenomena characterized by the abrupt entrance from without into consciousness of an idea or image ... which becomes a part of the stream of thought ..." temporarily— that is, the suggestion is accepted by the subject and acted upon or realized.

In hypnotic jargon, the word suggestion is used in its narrow sense to designate the things an operator says while inducing the hypnotic state, as well as the commands and orders he gives the already hypnotized subject. And by suggestibility is meant "the peculiar state of mind favorable to the acceptance of suggestion" (hypnosis) as well as the condition previous to induction (susceptibility or hypnotizability).

THE SUBCONSCIOUS MIND

There are two parts, or figuratively, two compartments in the human mind; for the sake of simplicity we might say that every person has two minds—the conscious, and the subconscious. When we are awake the conscious mind controls our actions, or most of them—we are awake or conscious. Those organs and parts of the body which we can control by the exercise of will, or volition, are under the jurisdiction of the conscious mind.

When we are asleep we are largely unconscious—the conscious mind is subdued or inactive. Any movements or actions that we perform while asleep are caused by the subconscious mind; dreams also are stirred up by subconscious activity. But during natural sleep the subconscious mind as well as the conscious is inaccessible from the outside. We might say that both minds are asleep, though not totally.

Under hypnosis, however, the conscious mind is rendered inactive and the subconscious awakened to a proportionate extent—the more unconscious the subject is, the deeper the hypnotic trance. In the hypnotic sleep the subconscious mind controls the entire organism, not the voluntary system alone, but also the involuntary nervous system. It is for this reason that mental and nervous ills can be cured through hypnosis.

A hypnotized person accepts most of the suggestions of the operator, excepting only those that might offend his sense of decency. The mind, being extremely plastic, is easily swayed, and through the mind all the functions of the body can be caused to undergo alteration and modification to a marked degree. The senses also can be rendered very acute, and conversely, the senses can be subdued so that the subject seems to become unaware of certain stimuli, such as pain, thus achieving a condition of anesthesia.

The actual nature of hypnosis is not yet known. Most authorities in the field are quick to admit they do not know exactly what hypnosis is. The several theories, which have been advanced through the years, are inadequate to explain the hypnotic phenomenon. In fact, all the theories put together do not answer all the questions that we have.

We hope that in the future some experimenter will be able to throw light on the subject.

LESSON EIGHT
INDUCTION TECHNIQUES

HOW TO HYPNOTIZE

To the uninitiated, the hypnotic induction process seems to consist of a mumbo jumbo of sleep talk. It seems to be very haphazard and aimless. Actually, the induction process has a very definite plan. We might say there is a design behind the induction method. I call this plan of induction the "three-step procedure."

The first step is the "preparatory or introductory step" in which the operator describes the signs or symptoms of approaching hypnosis. Speaking in the future tense, he tells the subject how he will become relaxed, how his arms and legs will become heavy, how his eyelids will begin to droop as his eyes become tired, how he will get drowsy and sleepy, how finally his eyelids will flutter and his eyes will close and how he will fall into a deep and sound sleep.

Everything is couched in terms of what will happen so that the subject begins to expect these things to happen. He is led along gradually. This process may take anywhere from a minute to four or five minutes.

The future tense suggestions are kept up until there are some signs that they are beginning to take effect. One of the signs, for example, is the narrowing of the eyes, the drooping of the eyelids. Another sign is a tendency for the body to sag. These are often obvious signs of relaxation. Then you are ready for the second step.

This step is called "talking sleep." You now begin to tell the subject how he is already feeling and you talk in the present tense, telling him that now his eyes are feeling tired and his eyelids are heavy and drooping, that his body is relaxed and is relaxing more and more, that every muscle is becoming loose and limp, that he is becoming drowsy and sleepy and tired, that it is difficult to keep his eyes open and that soon he will close them and fall into a deep sound, hypnotic sleep.

The second step is the main part of the induction procedure. It is kept up until the subject's eyes close. If the eyes close spontaneously, this is a good sign that he is going into hypnosis, so then you take the third step.

In the third step, you assume "control." If the subject's eyes close spontaneously, it is a good sign that he is going into hypnosis. Therefore you drop the monotonous patter, which is the main characteristic of the second step, and become firmer and more authoritative in your suggestions. You "take over." You assume "control." You tell him that now he is falling into a deep, sleep, deep and sound sleep, and he is now in effect under your "control."

To summarize, therefore, the three steps of the induction process are: first, the preparatory or introductory step consisting of a description of the symptoms the subject is about to experience. Second, the talking sleep step in which suggestions of sleep are repeated in the present tense as happening at the moment, and third, the step in which you assume the hypnotic control, when the monotonous stimulation of the sleep talk is quickly replaced by direct emphatic, unequivocal suggestions of sleep. These steps are Used in most of the ordinary methods of induction. In instantaneous methods and in very rapid inductions, the first two steps are usually eliminated.

Corresponding to the above three steps of induction, the subject goes through three mental phases.

In the past, the subject was told to *concentrate* on a spot or on the operator's voice. Concentration involves conscious effort and only the very best subjects are able through this method to go into hypnosis. This method has to work quickly. If it does not work in a few moments, the effort of concentration tends to produce an opposite reaction. It tends to produce fatigue so that the concentration and the attention drop and the subject's mind drifts off the attention spot. Therefore, for about 75% of subjects the concentration element is not only undesirable but actually hinders induction.

A far better technique to use is to induce the idea of "contention." Contention is a coined word and is actually a combination of several other ideas. It can be expressed as follows: The subject is told to look at a spot on the wall, for example; he is told to place his attention on this spot and not to remove his attention for a moment, not to let his eyes drift away from it. In other words, he is told to keep his attention focused or fixed on the object, but he is told to do it *easily, effortlessly,* that it isn't a hard task to keep one's attention on a spot. Contention can be expressed as a combination of attention and concentration of thought minus the effort that is usually involved in concentration. So we might call it, for the sake of simplicity, *effortless concentration.*

This is the first phase that the subject enters and it corresponds to the preparatory or introductory step of the operator; as he effortlessly concentrates upon a spot, the operator describes how he is going to feel and what symptoms he is going to experience as he approaches hypnosis. Gradually, the subject's attention becomes fixed on the object, but now completely without effort. It is very similar to the situation which we sometimes encounter in speaking of an orator, you often hear the remark "the audience was hanging on his words." The subject finds himself in a similar state of mind. He is hanging on the operator's words. His attention is hanging, fixed, spontaneously, completely without effort, on the fixation object. This condition is called *fixation* and sometimes *monoideism*. It is a condition in which one idea or train of thought prevails in the subject's mind: the idea of going into hypnosis. It is a completely effortless and spontaneous condition of fixed attention.

While the subject is in this phase, the operator is "talking sleep." This is the main part of the induction process. Then, as this phase progresses, the subject's eyes become very, very tired, and finally they flutter and close. As they close, the operator assumes control and the subject drops into a condition of complete passivity—a condition that corresponds to and becomes hypnosis as the operator "takes over." The taking over of control at this point produces the condition known as "rapport."

It is imperative that you understand the above three steps of the induction process. It is important for this reason: If you tell a subject prematurely that his eyes are tired, that he is drowsy and sleepy, in his own mind he thinks "Bud, you're a liar!" because he does not feel that way at all. He rejects that suggestion and tends to reject the suggestions that follow. Therefore, you must not tell him anything that is not true. You can give him a lot of possibilities of what *will* happen, but don't say that it is happening until you actually see evidence that it is. As pointed out earlier, some of the signs that the suggestions are starting to "take" are: deeper breathing, drooping of the eyelids, narrowing of the eyes, perhaps a slumping or slouching of the body, a tendency for the head to droop forward or to one side, etc.

When you point out something that is already occurring the subject develops confidence in you and thinks to himself—"This guy knows what he is talking about! I do feel that way!" and this leads him to accept the suggestions that follow and therefore steadily leads him into hypnosis.

THE "PURE" VERBAL SUGGESTION METHOD

The following is the verbal suggestion method in its pure form. It is very rarely used in this way. It is usually combined with counting or other devices, which tend to lend it more body and substance. However, the basis of most of the standard methods is verbal suggestion. Therefore, it is advisable that you familiarize yourself with this method. Notice especially, the gradual transition from the first to the second steps and then to the third. Notice also, how the subject is brought into the condition of contention. Be reminded that these transitions from step to step are to be made in such a way as to be imperceptible to the subject or to untrained observers.

With the subject in the proper position, whether seated or lying down, you place or hold a suitable object before him and proceed as follows:

"Now relax completely and place your attention on this object in front of you. Look at it steadily but without straining. Don't take your eyes away for a moment. Keep your attention focused on the object. Do so easily, effortlessly. It isn't much of a task to keep your attention but focused on this object. Now, as you gaze at it, your body will gradually and steadily become very, very relaxed. Your arms will relax, and your legs will relax. Gradually, a vague numbness and dullness will come over your arms and your legs. Your eyes will become rather tired as you gaze at this object. Your eyelids will get heavy. Gradually, your eyelids will droop and your eyes will slowly narrow down to slits. Your arms and legs will begin to feel this vague numbness and dullness. They will get more and more numb and dull and heavy as I go on. You will become drowsy, drowsy and sleepy. Your eyelids will get heavier and heavier. Your eyes will feel like closing. Your head may get heavy too. Your head may seem to droop forward or to one side. At some point your eyes will close; your eyelids may droop first, may flutter, and then your eyes will close, your head will fall forward on your chest possibly, or maybe to one side, and you will fall into a deep, sound sleep."

These and similar suggestions that will occur to you as you gain experience are repeated over and over again. Do not begin the second step until the subject is perfectly motionless and you begin to see some of the signs mentioned, and you have reason to believe that he is perfectly relaxed. Then continue:

"You are now completely relaxed, both in mind and body. Just let yourself go completely and soon you will be fast asleep. Your eyelids feel heavy now. They're droopy now. Drooping more and more. Your eyes are narrowing down to slits. Your arms and legs are getting that numb feeling I mentioned; your breathing is getting deeper and more regular. Your eyes feel very, very tired. Your eyelids feel heavy as lead. You are getting drowsy and sleepy, more drowsy and sleepy and tired as I go on. Your arms and legs are numb and dull. Your head feels heavy with sleep; your entire body is heavy with sleep. The object is becoming blurred and indistinct; your eyes are very tired and bleary. They may even start to tear somewhat. Your eyes feel like closing. It would feel so good to close your eyes and go into a deep, sound hypnotic sleep. You are getting more and more sleepy, very, very, sleepy— more and more sleepy and tired; your breathing is deep and regular, your head is heavy with sleep, arms and legs are numb and dull, entire body feels heavy with sleep, your eyelids feel heavy as lead, your eyes feel like closing. You're very, very sleepy, very sleepy; your eyelids are beginning to droop. It would feel so good to close your eyes. They are drooping more and more. Your eyelids are fluttering now—now they're closing, closing ... That's

31

right, close your eyes and go into a deep and sound sleep now! Deep and sound sleep!"

At this point, your voice becomes more firm, more authoritative and you keep on saying "deeper and deeper asleep," strongly, firmly, authoritatively. By this time, if your subject closed his eyes spontaneously, he is probably in hypnosis. But you cannot be too certain. In any case, it is better to take a little more time and try to put him into a deeper state. Therefore you continue, speaking in a slightly louder tone, rather emphatically and forcefully:

"You are now sound asleep but I shall put you into a deeper state still. I am going to count to ten. Every count will put you into a still deeper and deeper sleep, until finally when I say 'ten' you will be in a very deep and sound sleep and completely in hypnosis. You will obey all my commands implicitly. On the count of "ten" you will be deep asleep. Now—ONE!— you're going down deeper and deeper. Two!—you're sinking into a deeper and deeper hypnotic state. Three!—Four!—Five!—going deeper and deeper still. Six!—Seven!—letting go completely; going deep, deep, asleep! Eight—very deep and sound and restful hypnotic sleep! Nine!—deeper and deeper and deeper in hypnosis! Ten!—deep asleep, sound asleep! You are in a deep and sound hypnotic sleep!"

This ends the induction. Now the subject is usually tested to see whether he is actually under hypnosis. The test may be an eye catalepsy challenge or an arm catalepsy challenge. We will go into this phase later.

ADDITIONAL HYPNOTIC PHRASES

The suggestions in the above method can be varied in many ways, as you will learn through experience. The following are some additional, excellent, tried and tested hypnotic phrases.

"Gaze steadily at the disc, steadily and fixedly. Your eyes are tearing. It would feel so good to close them. Your head is lolling forward, heavy with sleep. Everything is going further and further away. Sleep is approaching. A dense cloud of sleep is enveloping you. It is very hard to keep your eyes open. They feel like closing. Every count is making you more drowsy and sleepy. More and more drowsy, sleepy, and tired. Every count seems to be forcing you deeper and deeper asleep. Your entire body seems numb and dull and devoid of sensation. You feel like you are floating in the air. Like you are swaying or rocking back and forth. Your mind has no thought except the one idea of sleep. You are falling deeper and deeper asleep," and so on.

PREPARATORY OR INTRODUCTORY TALK

In preparing subjects for induction, especially subjects who seem fearful or skeptical due to ignorance, it is wise to give them a rough idea of the nature of hypnosis. It may be explained that no possible harm can result from its application by an expert, that the hypnotic sleep is healthful and restful, and that there are untold advantages in its use. [t should be stressed that no one can be hypnotized against his will and that even in the deepest stages the subject will not respond to suggestions offensive to his moral principles. Explain the desirability and benefits of complete relaxation; a person must "let himself go" both in mind and body—he must be willing to be hypnotized. If he is Unwilling, either consciously or unconsciously, your efforts can be of no avail.

Taking the subject into your confidence in this manner will increase your prestige in his eyes and give him the feeling that you are indeed earnest and sincere, and an able hypnotist. Very often the most skeptical subject can be won over in this way, thus insuring a successful hypnosis.

SUBJECT'S POSITION

The subject may be seated or may lie down on a bed or couch. Actually the seated position is preferable because the recumbent position has a tendency to put a person into a natural sleep. Have the subject sit in a chair in such a way that his back is firmly supported. His feet should be flat on the floor in a position that will permit the thighs to be completely relaxed. Do not allow him to cross his knees or his ankles. As a person starts to go into hypnosis, and becomes completely relaxed, his body becomes very heavy. Should his legs be crossed, the weight of one leg upon the other can become so oppressive as to keep him from going into hypnosis. Do not allow him to rest his hands on his stomach or his chest. Have them resting either on the arms of the chair or lying loosely on his thighs. Make certain that he is comfortable in other ways, that his collar is loose and that his belt is eased. With many subjects, as they go into hypnosis the breathing seems to change from chest breathing to abdominal breathing so that tightness of the belt might cause constriction around the waist, interfering with the freedom of their breathing.

THE FIXATION OBJECT

The fixation object can be almost anything from a very simple spot on the wall to a complicated hypno-aid such as a revolving disc or a revolving mirror.

Today hypno-aids are available from various companies supplying hypnotists. Catalogs of hypno-aids are available on request.

Generally speaking, if a small fixation object such as a crystal ball is used, it should be held a dozen or so inches from the subject's eyes slightly above his eye level. Larger objects may be placed at proportionately greater distances from the subject. It is usually more convenient for the fixation object to be fixed on the wall or placed on some article of furniture so that the operator can stand slightly behind the subject and to one side in order to be out of the subject's range of vision, and yet in such a position that the side of the subject's face and one eye can be easily seen in order to note his responses.

METHODS OF AWAKENING

There are really many methods of awakening hypnotized subjects but at present we need concern ourselves with only one, the method that I consider most effective and best for beginners.

Tell the subject that you are about to awaken him. Impress upon him authoritatively that when he awakens he will feel quite all right in every way. State that you are going to count to five and when you say "five" he will be perfectly wide awake, feel fine in every respect, and even better than before he was hypnotized. Then say "One—two—three—four—five!—Wake up! You're wide awake!" quite sharply, and clap your hands or snap your fingers to emphasize your commands.

Never slap a subject's face to awaken him. And avoid awakening him suddenly; it is prefer-able that you induce expectation first, and then bring him out of it gradually by counting. Unless a subject is awakened properly, with suitable suggestions of health and general well-being given him previously, he is likely to experience headaches, eye-strain, or other discomforts after awakening.

LESSON NINE
INDUCTION TECHNIQUES
STANDARD METHODS
(Continued)

DR. FLOWER'S METHOD

The method that follows is a very easy method because it does not require much sustained and continued use of hypnotic patter. The method consists largely of counting. Whatever talking has to be done comprises the first or introductory step. The second step consists almost entirely of counting on the part of the operator and opening and closing of the eyes on the part of the subject. Therefore it is a method in which the subject actively participates.

Seat your subject in the usual position, but facing a blank wall or door. You stand behind him and slightly to one side. In this position you are able to see the side of his face and one eye so that you can closely observe his reactions. In this method, fixation of the eyes on a particular object is not required. Begin as follows:

"Just relax and look at the wall or door in front of you in a vague, general, dreamy sort of way. In a little while, I will begin to count. On each count I want you to close your eyes and between counts open them, in this manner." Get in front of him and illustrate the procedure that you want him to follow. Count "one," and shut your eyes for a second, then open them. Say "two," close your eyes again and open them again. Say "three," and repeat the procedure. On the third count pretend that it is becoming difficult for you to open your eyes, as if you're opening them with an effort, thus lending added strength to this suggestion.

Resume your position behind him and continue. You will keep on closing your eyes on every count, and opening them between counts until they get very tired. It will become more and more difficult to reopen your eyes each time and you will get drowsy and sleepy as you continue. Every time you close your eyes, it will seem to become still more and more difficult to open them. You will become more and more reluctant to open your eyes between counts. As you continue in this fashion, your arms will get heavy and your legs will get heavy. Your entire body will become more and more relaxed. Finally you will be so sleepy and tired, it'll be so difficult to reopen your eyes between counts that you won't bother anymore. At some point along the way, you will just close them and leave them closed and go into a deep, sound sleep."

Having explained what the subject is to expect (Step One), begin to count evenly and monotonously. Count up to twenty and if his eyes still have not closed, continue counting, going back to one and around to twenty again. Continue in series of twenty until hypnosis results. A good subject will close his eyes perhaps even before you reach fifteen. The first indication is usually a noticeable effort in opening the eyes. Also, there is often a loss of coordination so that the opening and the closing of the eyes are not in time with your counting. When they finally remain closed altogether, you can often observe a raising and lowering of the eyebrows as if the subject is continuing to make vain efforts to open his eyes between the counts.

Once his eyes are closed, you stop counting and make emphatic suggestions that he is now

35

going into hypnosis (Step Three). If you wish, you may continue to count until you reach twenty but now each count is associated with deepening suggestions. You tell him that on each count he is going deeper and deeper into hypnosis and finally when you reach the count of twenty, you become especially firm and authoritative, and take over. Assume control as is required in the third step.

Sometimes the subject's eyes don't close, but co-ordination becomes so impaired that it is not necessary to wait until they close. Therefore, when you reach twenty, if the coordination is extremely impaired, stop counting and take over control and give him emphatic suggestions that he is going deep into hypnosis.

If he has not closed his eyes after you have completed three series of twenty, and if there isn't a definite impairment of coordination, then you can assume that the method isn't working. But it isn't wise to stop in the middle of a method. In this case, therefore, when you reach the third twenty, tell him to close his eyes and relax and then proceed with a relaxation method or with any other method which can be continued with the eyes closed. The average subject will not even realize that you are switching methods. He will just assume that this is the way you ordinarily operate.

There are three common variations in Dr. Flower's Method. The first is the spontaneous closing of the eyes, at which point the operator takes over control. Second is the impairment of coordination in opening and closing of the eyes, making it logical to tell him to close them and taking over at that point; and third, when it's obvious the method isn't working, switching to another method.

INTERMITTENT COUNTING AND SUGGESTION METHOD

This method employs the frequency principle of suggestion rather than the repetition principle. That is, repetitions of sleep suggestions are broken up with counting. The frequency principle is generally more effective than the repetition principle.

In the first step, explain to the subject that you are going to count to twenty and that on every count he will get more and more sleepy, etc. This introductory phase is kept up for several minutes while the subject gazes at the fixation point, as in the verbal suggestion method. The fixation object can be almost anything you care to select. You do not start the second step until there are signs that some of the reactions that you are describing are beginning to work. Examples: the drooping of the eyelids, sagging of the head, the appearance of relaxation of the body. When you feel the time is ripe for the second step you begin to count as follows:

"One, two, three, four—you are getting more and more relaxed on every count. Your eyes are becoming rather tired and your eyelids are beginning to droop. Five, six— more and more tired on each and every count. You are becoming drowsy, drowsy and sleepy. Seven, eight, nine— more tired on each and every count. Your arms and legs are developing a vague numbness and dullness, a strange heaviness. Your entire body is becoming heavy with sleep. Ten—very heavy and very, very tired. Your breathing is becoming deeper and more regular. Eleven, twelve—very, very, tired and sleepy. Your arms are so heavy and your legs are so heavy. Your entire body is very heavy and relaxed. Your breathing is deeper and more regular. Your eyelids are becoming heavier as I go on. Fourteen, fifteen—it's becoming difficult to keep your eyes open. When I say twenty, your eyes will close and you will drop into a deep, sound and restful sleep. Sixteen—very, very tired, very, very sleepy. Seventeen—your eyes are starting to close. It's becoming difficult to keep them open now. Twenty!—and go into a deep, sound and restful sleep! Very, very deep, very sound and restful sleep!"

Sometimes, shortly after you begin to count, if you notice that it's becoming difficult for him to keep his eyes open, you might inject the suggestion that "your eyes will close on the count of twenty and possibly even before." This will cause him to close his eyes anytime rather than forcing him to wait for the count of twenty. Therefore, if his eyes close before you reach twenty, you take over at that point. You continue counting to twenty but each count then becomes a deepener, rather than a part of the original induction procedure.

The idea, then, is to interrupt the counting with verbal suggestion as in the very first method, gradually building up the subject's expectation of going into hypnosis on the count of twenty. This is why you should keep on repeating:

"Every count is making you more and more sleepy. On the count of twenty your eyes will close, your head will fall forward," etc. The count of twenty is a signal which the subject is made to anticipate—the psychological moment at which point he will be projected into hypnosis.

If, when you reach about fifteen or sixteen, there are no indications that his eyes are becoming tired, it may be advisable to change your line somewhat. So rather than saying, "on the count of twenty your eyes will close," say, "you will permit your eyes to close," thereby leaving you an opening so that when you reach twenty, if his eyes don't close spontaneously, he will know he is expected to close them voluntarily. If this is the case you have no right to expect that he is now in hypnosis. This, therefore, is a time when you again have to shift to another method. Here again, you might change to the Progressive Relaxation method or to any other method in which you can proceed with the eyes already closed. Or you can continue with intermittent counting and suggestion, saying now, "I'm going to count from one to ten. On the count of ten you will go into a deep, sound, hypnotic state." And you continue counting—interrupting the count with suggestions. If you wish, you can then go into a series of five, telling him that on the count of five he will drop into hypnosis. You continue in this way until you have some inkling that he is in hypnosis; then you test to determine if he actually is under.

When you reach the signal counts such as "twenty," "ten," "five," you become more emphatic and authoritative because this marks the beginning of the third step at which you take over control. The intermittent counting and suggesting constitute the second step.

The above methods are not single methods in themselves. Each one is a combination of two, three, or more other methods. A hypnotist who learns the above three methods thoroughly and can apply them expertly, can consider himself fairly well equipped. It must be borne in mind, however, that no one method can be effective to a like degree on all subjects. Individual psychological differences must be taken into consideration and methods used to suit particular cases. This can be best accomplished through experience.

THE CHALLENGE

When you think a person is in hypnosis and you do the first test to determine that he is, this is called a challenge. The simplest and easiest challenge to do at the beginning is the "Eye Catalepsy Challenge." Regardless of what method you use, when you are ready for the challenge, you proceed as follows:

"Your eyes are closed and the muscles around your eyes are flaccid, loose, limp, and relaxed. Your eyes are tightly shut, and you cannot open them but don't try. Don't try until I count to three. On the count of three, you will try to open your eyes but you will not be able to do so. Your eyes will be stuck, glued together, and you will not be able to open them.

On the count of three you will try to open your eyes but you will not be able to do so. If you make a strong effort you may be able to raise your eyebrows, because a different set of muscles, a larger set, is involved in raising the eyebrows, but you cannot raise your eyelids. It is as if you have forgotten how to move the appropriate muscle. You simply cannot open your eyes.

"Now ONE!—your eyes are stuck and you cannot open them! TWO!—they're glued tightly together and you cannot open them! THREE!—you cannot open them! Try, but you cannot! Stop trying! And now go deeper and deeper into a hypnotic state."

You must not give the subject too much of a chance with the first challenge. A few seconds is sufficient. If he cannot open his eyes in a few seconds don't let him try any longer because if he makes a continued effort, he may eventually open them. The first test is very precarious. You don't really know whether or not the subject is under or how deep he is. Many a subject has been "lost" because of the improper performance of the first test or challenge. If the first test has worked out well, in the second one you can allow him to try a little longer.

The second test is the Arm Catalepsy Test. Raise his arm, stretch it out, and give it a slight tug as if you intend in this way to make it rigid. At the same time tell him, "Your arm is now becoming cataleptic. The muscles inside are tensing up. Your arm is stuck, it's rigid, and it's cataleptic! You cannot move your arm! You cannot lower it! When I say three, you will try to lower your arm but you will not be able to do so. If you try to push it down, it will bounce back. Now, ONE!—your arm is stuck and you cannot lower it. TWO!—you cannot lower your arm. THREE!— you cannot lower it! Try to lower it but you cannot do so! Try hard but you cannot do it! Now stop trying and go into a deeper hypnosis! And now, as I loosen up your arm and put it down into your lap, you go into a still deeper hypnosis!"

Suiting action to your words, you take hold of his arm, you loosen up the elbow, loosen up the shoulders, slowly lower it, at the same time telling him to go deeper and deeper into hypnosis.

EMERGENCY METHODS OF AWAKENING

Should a subject fail to awaken promptly through the ordinary method, which is a very rare occurrence, it is usually either because he enjoys the complete relaxation of hypnotic sleep and wishes to continue it, or because of a preconceived fear that he will not awaken.

Do not lose your self-assurance. Determine what the reason is through questioning. Explain that his fears are unfounded and impress upon him the desirability of awakening. Or state that he has rested sufficiently and is now ready to awaken. On the count of "Five!" he is to be wide awake. Then proceed as in the ordinary method. The actual awakening can be varied in an interesting manner by having the subject himself do the counting and awaken as he does so. He may also be told to take a deep breath on each count.

Sometimes blowing sharply on his closed eyes will awaken a subject. Also you may raise the lids and blow short, sharp breaths into the naked eyes.

Should all these methods fail, which is rare indeed, merely place the subject on a bed or couch, instruct him to sleep until he feels like awakening, and leave him. In due time he will awaken of his own accord. In no case can any harm result in this respect, if you do not become alarmed.

In extreme cases, place a small fan in front of the subject, prop his eyes open, and allow the cool air to hit his face and eyes. Should a certain amount of lassitude continue, get him on his feet and walk him briskly about in the open air to stimulate circulation.

LESSON TEN

INDUCTION TECHNIQUES

(Continued)

BASIC METHODS

Mesmeric methods include all the methods in which are employed "passes" with or without contact, so called after Franz Anton Mesmer, the originator of animal magnetism, or mesmerism. Mesmerism itself is now obsolete and useless because of the erroneous principles on which it was founded, but passes are still used by many hypnotists as aids to induction.

Passes without contact are made by moving the palms and fingers of your hands downwards across the subject's face and body without actually touching him. These passes should be made quite slowly, beginning over the top of the head and continuing, always downward, over the face and chest, and, if the subject is in a recumbent position, along the abdomen, hips and legs. Passes are repeated continuously while at the same time verbal suggestions of sleep are made. In most cases passes should be made only after the eyes are closed.

Passes with contact are usually limited to the face. They are made downward with the fingers across the forehead from the hairline to the bridge of the nose, or outward from the center of the forehead and along the temples. It takes practice to be able to make passes with contact in a suitable manner; beginners should limit themselves to suggestion methods and no-contact passes.

It must be stressed that passes have no real value. They are simple indirect suggestions and their effect might be termed a "placebo" effect. Many hypnotists never use them at all.

Liebeault's Method. This consisted of holding the forefinger and middle fingers of the right hand about two feet from the subject's face, and while making suggestions, gradually bringing them closer and closer. When the fingers are almost touching the subject's eyes, his lids droop and his eyes close. A few commands of "Sleep!" usually sufficed to bring him under control.

Bernheim's Method Hypolyte Bernheim, Liebeault's pupil and head of the Nancy School, also used two fingers, but only for concentration of attention. The test of the method consisted entirely of verbal suggestion.

Braid's Method. James Braid, the inventor of the word "hypnosis," used the bright reflection of light on his surgeon's scalpel as an object for fixation. He believed fixation to be of the utmost importance, though he used verbal suggestion as well.

Candle Method. This consists of having the subject stare at the flickering flame of a candle while the operator makes suggestions. Although very effective, this method is undesirable because its use may result in headaches upon awakening.

Professor Cook's Method The method of Professor William W. Cook differs from the ordinary methods in that the subject is himself required to hold the hypno-disc before his eyes. He holds it in one hand by means of a handle attached to the back of the disk. After a few minutes, during which time the subject becomes very fatigued, the operator relieves him of the task of holding the disk, and continues in the usual manner, using suggestions in conjunction.

Luy's Method Dr. Luy used a mechanism called the "Revolving Mirror" for fixation. This comprised two small mirrors mounted on the ends of a short horizontal bar, which in turn was fixed to a vertical bar, making a figure T. The foot of the T was mounted on a base, which revolved by clockwork. The "Revolving Mirror" forms the basis of many similar mechanisms employed as aids to induction. Some operators employ sound mechanisms, such as metronomes, to supply continuous auditory stimulation. Recordings of entire sleep-suggestion methods are often used to make the hypnotist's task easier and to hypnotize people without his presence. Recordings, however, will not influence a sufficient percentage of subjects, probably because of the absence of the necessary personal prestige of the operator.

Vilk's Method Though using many methods, Dr. Eduard Vilk deserves credit for originating the so-called "religious" methods. These can be applied with good results to devoutly religious subjects. Both fixation and suggestion are necessary in this type of method; the only real differences are the operator's pious mien and his use of "thee" and "thou" forms in making suggestions.

Method for Bald-Headed Subjects. Dr. X. Lamontte Sage considered the following method effective with bald headed men and others with high or receding hairlines. The subject is seated as usual, with his eyes closed at the start. the operator stands before him and, with the first three fingers of his right hand, taps him gently on the head just above where his hairline normally would have been. This tapping should continue steadily and without interruption at about one second intervals, the operator meanwhile keeping up a running stream of suggestions, until hypnosis is induced. This method is based on the metronome method in which auditory stimulation supplied by the ticking of the metronome causes hypnosis. Here, the tapping supplied not only the sensory stimulation, but also the "touch object" (instead of the sight-object or hypno-disc) for the purpose of fixation. Thus, you should understand that fixation does not apply merely to the sense of sight, by using a disk, but also to the sense of hearing as with the metronome, or the sense of touch, as exemplified by tapping. (Mesmeric passes are also in this class). Of course, two or more types of fixation may be used simultaneously. Optic fixation upon a hypno-disc and auditory fixation upon a metronome's ticking are good examples of multiple fixations.

METHODS OF THE OLD MASTERS
SIMPLE BUT EFFECTIVE

It should be noted that the basic methods as used by the old masters were extremely effective in spite of being very rudimentary. Apparently they were able to produce hypnosis much more quickly with a larger proportion of subjects that it is possible today. Undoubtedly this was due to the fact the subjects in those days were "unsophisticated." Today, everybody knows a little about everything, psychology and hypnosis included. Therefore, this has taken the edge off their suggestibility. They don't just believe implicitly. They have to know why everything happens. This tendency to question is responsible for the tendency to resist hypnosis.

Also in those days a professional man exercised much more prestige than he does today. A doctor was someone to be reckoned with. Today a doctor is just another "Good Joe."

Modern methods, therefore, are much more complex and yet, in spite of this complexity, they are not as effective today as the very simple methods of the past were.

LESSON ELEVEN
STAGES OF HYPNOSIS

There are almost as many systems for dividing hypnosis into stages or levels as there are operators. The Davis and Husband Susceptibility Scoring System has thirty divisions, and another, the LeCron-Bordeaux Scoring System, has fifty. Other systems contain three to nine divisions. I have found, however, that dividing hypnosis into six stages gives us an adequate and workable system for all practical purposes. These stages are as follows:

1. Hypnoidal or Lethargic Stage
2. Light Sleep
3. Sleep
4. Deep Sleep
5. Somnambulism
6. Profound Somnambulism

The first three are termed mnesic (memory-retaining) stages while the last three are amnesic (no-memory) stages.

The first three stages are characterized by a greatly varying degree of consciousness or awareness of the surroundings. Upon awakening the subject usually remembers all that transpired in the trance. In the first two stages the subject may be unable to open his eyes upon challenge and may also be unable to bend or lower his arm if told he cannot do so (partial catalepsy). In the third stage there is fairly good control of the voluntary muscular system; the subject will be unable to activate any muscle or group of muscles so that he will be unable to rise or sit down, he will be unable to speak if told he cannot use his organs of speech and he will be unable to articulate specific words or sounds upon appropriate command. Thus, if told to count and forget a certain number, he will be unable to utter that number, but he will not have forgotten it in the third stage. Only negligible post-hypnotic reactions are possible in the first and second stages. Upon awakening the subject is likely to express doubt that he was hypnotized at all. It is quite common to hear him say, "I could have opened my eyes (or lowered my arm, etc.) had I tried a little harder." (As if it takes any effort to perform these simple actions!)

In the third stage it is possible to produce glove or partial analgesia (insensitivity to pain), partial or fragmentary amnesia, and incomplete hallucinations (visualization) of some of the senses with the eyes closed; having the subject open his eyes in this stage may result in awakening. Post-hypnotic suggestions involving fairly simple actions will be performed. Temporary, fragmentary amnesia may exist in some subjects after they awaken if strong suggestions to that effect are made.

The fourth stage is the beginning of the amnesic stages. A subject will forget a number, his name and almost anything else that is suggested to him. Upon awakening he will be unable to recall the events of the trance for possibly several hours. It is possible to produce analgesia so that he will not feel any pain stimuli, but he will retain the ability to feel the sensation or touch; thus, a severe pinch may be felt as a slight pressure. His eyes can be opened without danger of awakening him. Smell and taste hallucinations can be created. Post-hypnotic suggestions will be carried out. Hypermnesia may be developed. The hypnotic state can be reinduced upon a post-hypnotic command or signal; similarly, the subject himself may reinduce the trance by self-administration of a post-hypnotic signal.

The fifth is the beginning of the somnambulic stages. Complete anesthesia can be induced so that the subject will deny feeling any sensation whatsoever. Complete or selective amnesia is possible, both hypnotically and in the post-hypnotic state. Both positive and sometimes negative hallucinations are possible in the fifth stage. The sixth stage is profound somnambulism in which all the phenomena of hypnosis, including negative hallucinations (the subject does not see or hear people or things that are present), are manifested.

JUDGING HYPNOTIC DEPTH

To decide the depth of any given hypnotic state, one starts with the simpler experiments, increasing their complexity gradually until there are indications that the subject can go no further. For example, a subject's arm is made cataleptic and he is told he cannot lower it; if he lowers it, albeit with some difficulty, he is only in the first stage, providing he has been unable to open his eyes. Should he be unable to lower his arm, he is judged to be in at least the second stage. Then he is told to count to ten, forgetting the number between 5 and 7. Should he hesitate at that point for a while, with the obvious but futile effort to form the word "six," it can be concluded that he did not say t only because of muscular inability to do so (stage 3); the effort involved makes it plain that he did not forget the number. To further substantiate the stage, analgesia is attempted. If he has a slight degree of insensibility to pain stimuli, it is fairly certain he is in the third stage.

If, upon the suggestion that he has forgotten a certain number, the subject counts right through without appreciable pause, it can be assumed that he has amnesia for that number. To make doubly certain, it is advisable to suggest amnesia of his name, or his address. With the fact of amnesia established, it can be concluded that he is in at least the fourth stage, in which it is possible to produce complete analgesia, perhaps hallucinations, and have the subject open his eyes without impairing the trance. Should all the above phenomena manifest themselves, it is certain that he will also have a good degree of post-hypnotic amnesia and will be able to hypnotize himself soon after awakening upon self-administration of a post-hypnotic signal.

Beyond the fourth stage we have the somnambulic stages. To decide whether a subject is in somnambulism, he can be given the suggestion that he feels no pain and not even a touch upon stimulation. Should he feel nothing, he is in at least the fifth stage, or somnambulism. To decide whether he is in the sixth stage or profound somnambulism, one may experiment with negative hallucinations. Occasional subjects manifest negative visual hallucinations in the fifth stage, but when both visual and auditory negative hallucinations are easily produced, it may be said that the subject is in the stage of profound somnambulism. In this level all the phenomena of hypnosis may be produced, barring personality difficulties, which may obviate some manifestations of deep trance. For example, some subjects never have complete amnesia because of morbid fear of losing contact with the surroundings. Others may not permit themselves to have anesthesia, while some may have anesthesia for one type of stimulus but not for another. One of my subjects, an excellent somnambule, would permit a major operation under hypnotic anesthesia but reacts violently when a lighter or match is struck. Upon questioning, it was discovered that this subject, at the age of six, experienced a great fright during a fire, and this accounts for her unusual behavior under hypnosis; she becomes disturbed at the mere sound of a match being struck, in spite of strong hypnotic suggestions to the contrary.

ALL DIVISIONS OF HYPNOSIS ARE ARBITRARY

It cannot be stressed too strongly that the divisions of hypnosis are not exact. It is impossible to set up hard and fast rules in hypnosis. There is considerable overlapping of stages, and care must be exercised not to assume that just because one phenomenon is present, or because one is absent, a definite decision can be made on that flimsy basis as to exactly which stage exists. Two or more phenomena should be used as criteria, if possible, and individual differences should be taken into account. Some subjects, for example, can manifest hallucinations in earlier stages than expected, and some manifest hallucinations of certain senses, such as the olfactory or gustatory senses, before they will react to suggestions of tactile or auditory changes. It takes skill and knowledge to become proficient in judging depth of hypnosis; an open mind and keen powers of observation are helpful in developing this proficiency.

LESSON TWELVE
PHENOMENA OF HYPNOSIS

The phenomena of hypnosis fall into seven general categories. In this lesson these categories are outlined and specific examples are given with numbers in parenthesis after each experiment specifying the stage of hypnosis in which a specific hypnotic phenomenon can be produced. By referring to this lesson occasionally, the student will be reminded that it is important to know the stages of hypnosis n order to be able to decide what type of phenomenon can be produced in a specified level. Thus the subject responses that he is not capable of performing in the level that exists.

1—*Control of the Voluntary System*
A—Simple Muscular Control—eyelid catalepsy (No. 1), arm catalepsy (No. 2), clenched fist (No. 2), unable to raise arm (No. 2), etc.
B—Muscular and Simple Functional Control— inability to rise from chair (No. 3), inability to walk from spot (No. 3), revolving arms and inability to stop them (No. 3), etc.;
Aphasia—inability to articulate name or number (No. 3)

2—*Amnesia*
Inability to remember number, name, address, etc. (No. 4), inability to remember events of the trance (No. 4)

3—*Analgesia and Anesthesia*
Insensibility to pain (No. 4), insensibility to sensation or feeling as well as to pain (No. 5)

4—*Hallucinations*
A—Positive Hallucinations—seeing or hearing something that is not here (No. 5)
B—Negative Hallucinations—inability to see or to hear something that is there (No. 6)
The above four categories have been discussed in the previous lesson under *Stages Of Hypnosis* and for that reason appear in outline form. The categories that follow have not yet been discussed and will receive a little more attention.

5—*Hypermnesia*
Hypermnesia refers to the ability to remember better, recall more, and generally is considered to be the opposite of amnesia. There are three different types of hypermnesia experiments common to hypnosis.

A—Recall of incidents which have been consciously forgotten (No. 4 and occasionally No. 3). If a person is told to remember the name of his first-grade teacher while he is under hypnosis, he is likely to be able to do so even though in the waking state he has forgotten that name. He may be told to remember many other details of his early life and childhood, which he is likable to do in the waking state. In other words, a hypnotized person can brush aside the shroud of accumulated experiences and get behind them to events of the past, which have long been consciously forgotten.

B—Age Regression—reliving past events (No. 5 and No. 6)

Age regression is a rather remarkable phenomenon in which the subject is apparently able to relive events of the past with all the feeling and emotion that was attached to those experiences. Sometimes, if he is regressed to a childhood period, he may even speak like a child and behave like one. Thus, if you wanted a person to remember the name of his first-grade teacher through age regression, you could tell him that he is now sitting in his classroom and you could ask him to name the children who are around him. He could then tell you who is up in front at the desk, whether it is a man or a woman, what he or she looks like and also to give that person's name. He would reply in the present tense, acting in every way as if he were actually reliving that experience at the present time.

Age regression is an important tool for the therapist. It should not be played around with and induced without good reason; and it certainly should not be used in stage performances.

C—Photographic Memory (No. 5 and No. 6 with certain subjects).

Some subjects are able to perform feats of memory, which are extremely remarkable. Thus, a subject may be told to look at one side of a room, to close his eyes immediately and to recite all the objects that he saw on that side of the room. Or, he may be told to look at a page in a book, to close the book and to read the tenth line. If he has a photographic memory he may be able to do it with remarkable accuracy. A photographic memory is not something that a person can achieve or develop. It is a talent that some people have and most people have not. It is extremely rare. In my experience, I have seen only four cases of true photographic memory. An ordinary hypnotized subject can be helped to improve his memory through hypnosis, but he can not produce feats of photographic memory to any great extent.

6—*Sensory Hyperesthesia* (exaltation of the senses)*

Experiments in increasing acuity of the five senses vary with the subject and with the sense involved. Some of the senses can be modified in as early as the third stage, while others cannot be changed till a person reaches somnambulism. Because of the variations in response, sensory Hyperesthesia is not reliable as a criterion for judging a person's depth of trance. *Modifications of the visual and auditory senses have been discussed under heading of "Hallucinations."

A—Olfactory Sense

A subject's sense of smell can be modified so greatly that if you tell him a bottle of water smells like perfume, it may be so. Also, a bottle of ammonia may be held under his nose with a suggestion that it is perfume, and he will smell it with apparent enjoyment.

B—Gustatory Sense

A person's sense of taste can be so modified, that a glass of water may taste like wine. Drinking this water may actually intoxicate him

C—Tactile Sense

Actually, a negative hallucination of the tactile sense produces analgesia and anesthesia— the person's sense of touch is nullified. However, his sense of touch can often be made much more acute so that he can be made to feel that the touch of a pencil is a touch with a hot iron and the subject will jump at such contact. Or his fingertips can be rendered very acute so that if he rests them on a piece of cloth, it may seem to him that he feels the texture of the cloth under his fingers.

7—Modification of Physical Functions

By suggestion, a subject's respiration may be modified, causing his breathing to come faster or slower. Also, his heart action and pulse rate can be similarly changed. Peristaltic action can be stimulated and flow of gastric juices increased. Bleeding can be greatly reduced, and salivation increased or minimized. Experiments of this type should be conducted under medical supervision whenever possible.

8—Post-hypnotic Phenomena

Post-hypnotic suggestions become effective beginning with the second stage of hypnosis. In the second stage, only those phenomena, which can be produced at that level, can be projected into the subsequent waking state. However, this works for brief periods only.

Were it not for the phenomenon of post-hypnotic, hypnosis would be about as good as a sleeping pill. The effect would prevail only while the person was hypnotized. Immediately upon awakening, it would be dispelled. Therefore, it is important for us to understand post-hypnotic suggestion and its various types in order to be able to make the greatest use of them in our work with hypnosis.

Post-hypnotic suggestion may be divided into two types. The first is the kind that is projected or continued from hypnosis into the waking state. For example, a person is told that he has forgotten his name and even after he awakens, he will continue not to know his name until a specific signal is given or until a specified time has elapsed. When he wakes up, therefore, he will not know who he is. The suggestion is continued or projected from hypnosis right into the waking state. He is wide-awake in all respects except that he does not remember his name.

In the other type, the hypnotic effect is elicited in the waking state upon a signal arranged while the person is under hypnosis. Using the same example, we might describe this condition as follows: The subject is told under hypnosis that he does not know who he is. Then his name is given back to him—and then he is told, before he is awakened, perfectly normal in every way; he knows who he is, and then when the operator claps his hands twice, he suddenly loses his name again.

In the latter example, the clapping of the hands is a signal that awakens a subconscious impulse, the hypnotic suggestion, and the subject reacts with amnesia for his name.

The second type of post-hypnotic suggestion is more effective than the first in the sense that it can be made to persist for a longer period of time. Let me give you an example of a more practical type.

A subject is conditioned for dentistry. He is hypnotized and it is found that he has a sufficient degree of analgesia for the extraction of a tooth. He is hypnotized in the hypnotist's office and then sent to the dentist's office for the actual dental work. The trip from one office to the other may take as much as half an hour. If the first type of post-hypnotic suggestion is used, that is, if he is told that his jaw is numb and will continue to be numb until after he has reached the dentist's office and completed his work, the numbness may or may not last that long. Since the analgesia is in effect throughout his trip from one office to the other, it is gradually wearing out. The effect is gradually dissipating so that by the time he reaches the dentist's office, it may be gone or greatly diminished. When you use the second type of post-hypnotic suggestion, it works in this way: The subject is told when he wakes from hypnosis that he will be normal in every way and that there will be no numbness in his jaw at all. However, he is told that when he reaches the dentist's office and sits in his chair, all he needs to do is rub his jaw with his hand, whereupon the anesthesia will immediately return. In most cases, the anesthesia recurs in its full force and not in a dissipated or modified form.

Post-hypnotic suggestion is responsible for the many benefits that can accrue to us through hypnosis. Post-hypnotic suggestion is the principle that is employed in therapy. The therapeutic suggestion is made to continue over a period of time and its activity persists through repetition by the operator or by the subject himself In improving memory, concentration power, and other personal qualities, post-hypnotic suggestion is the key. In the breaking of habits, post-hypnotic suggestion is the major factor in bringing about such corrections. In short, post-hypnotic suggestion is the power that makes hypnotic influence persist and become permanent with the proper technique.

RELEASE FROM POST-HYPNOTIC CONTROL

Every post-hypnotic suggestion given with the intention of being temporary should be accompanied by its release. For example, if you tell your subject that after awakening he will be unable to light a cigarette with a match, he will indeed, upon awakening, be unable to bring his arm close enough to light the cigarette. His arms will stiffen and he will not be able to bring the flame near enough. This inability may persist for several hours or possibly for the rest of the day unless a signal releasing him from it is given. A satisfactory release may be a clap of the hands, a cough, a snap of the fingers, or a time limit. Be sure to remember just which release was arranged to terminate the post-hypnotic behavior. If you become confused and give the wrong release, it will of course not work. It has occurred in a number of instances that the subject was given a suggestion to have anesthesia upon awakening. Unless this suggestion is removed, the anesthesia tends to persist for a period of time proportionate with the depth of the trance. Although it will eventually wear off, the subject may become alarmed at the numbness and the alarm may recharge the post-hypnotic suggestion and cause it to last longer than it normally would.

AUTOHYPNOSIS OR SELF-HYPNOSIS

There are comparatively few cases on record where people have succeeded in actually hypnotizing themselves without the help of an outside agent. However, it is quite possible for a good hypnotic subject to be trained to induce self-hypnosis. The best way of accomplishing this is through post-hypnotic suggestion. A heterohypnotic state is required to begin with. Then the subject is merely given post-hypnotic suggestions repeatedly over a period of time to the effect that thereafter he will fall into hypnosis without the presence or aid of the hypnotist at some specified signal that he give himself. For example, he might count to ten, he might take four or five deep breaths; the counting or the breaths are the post-hypnotic signals to induce self-hypnosis. In order to awaken at a certain time, the subject merely thinks before he hypnotizes himself of the particular time when he wants to awaken and, lo and behold, he awakens at that time. A better way is to also give himself a signal for the awakening. Thus, when a time elapses, he can count back from five to one, or merely take a few more deep breaths, whereupon he awakens as per signal. Thus it should be easy to see how all important the phenomenon of post-hypnotic suggestion actually is.

LESSON THIRTEEN
ADVANCED METHODS

PERMISSIVE INDUCTION TECHNIQUES

Thus far we have discussed the standard methods of induction, which have been used for many years. In these standard methods, the subject externalizes his attention. He focuses upon or concentrates upon some thing or some one outside himself This may be the operator's voice, it may be the operator's fingers, or it may be an object the operator is holding or to which he calls the subject's attention. The idea is to attract the subject so much to the external object, that he becomes largely unaware of himself, so that the suggestions go readily into the subconscious.

As a result of the last two wars, some of the doctors who were forced to use hypnosis while in the service continued to use these techniques after getting back into private practice. Among these doctors were a small group of psychoanalysts. Psychoanalysis is a non-directive technique in which the patient is not told what to do. The patient lies on a couch usually, and talks freely—this is called free association. The doctor is not supposed to give him any directions and actually is not even supposed to answer any questions directly. He assumes an "unstructured" personality. If the patient asks a question, the doctor will usually counter with another question. This may sound extreme, but it is nonetheless true of the orthodox psychoanalytic methods.

These doctors were forced by necessity to use hypnotic techniques in the military service. Upon getting back into private practice it seemed a shame to drop these techniques. They wanted to continue them but they were reluctant to do so because this would run counter to their way of working in psychoanalytic practice.

A few of the more courageous of the analysts finally worked out a little system through which they were able to induce hypnosis in their patients, apparently without giving the patient any commands or direct suggestions. They did it by having the subject contemplate himself internally, so to speak, rather than contemplating an object externally as in the standard methods. Thus they would call attention to the way he felt, physically and mentally. They would call attention to his breathing, to the movements of his chest, the circulation of the blood, and to certain minor physical reactions, which are termed sensorimotor reactions. Gradually, by extending this process, they got the person into hypnosis. The following method is an illustration of the permissive approach to the induction of hypnosis.

The subject is usually seated in a comfortable position and the operator is also seated in front of him or perhaps somewhat to one side. There is no hootin' and hollerin' on the part of the operator; there are no commands, no direct statements—in the beginning at least—of any sort. The operator speaks slowly, calmly, and somewhat in this vein:

"As you sit there comfortably, look down in the general direction of your hands. If you wish, you can look at your right hand, or if you prefer, at the left hand. Or perhaps you would much rather look between your hands, at your thighs or down at the floor. Don't look at any particular spot but just in the vague, general area and direction of your hands.

"You probably think that you are sitting motionless, but actually you are not. As I shall point out to you, no living human being is completely motionless. There is always something going on in the body. The heart is always beating. Ordinarily you aren't aware of the beating of your heart because you aren't paying any attention to it, but if you think of your heart beating, not only can you feel it, but you can sometimes even hear it. Your lungs are always contracting and expanding, of course on an unconscious level. But if you think of the action of your lungs, you can actually feel the expansion and contraction of your chest.

"In a minor way, the circulation of your blood is also something you can become aware of if you think of it. You may actually feel the way your blood courses through your veins. In a minor sense still, as you look down on any part of your body, as you contemplate any part of your body, you are about to notice little reactions, which you wouldn't notice if you didn't contemplate that area. For example, since you are looking in the general direction of your hands you probably will notice little reactions developing in them. One or the other hand will start out very shortly with some sort of reaction. You might feel a tingle or a twitch in some part of either hand. For example, one of the fingers of your right hand might move slightly, might twitch, or of course, it might be your left hand. Instead of a twitch there might be another kind of reaction. You might feel a little tingling sensation or an itch some-where on the hand; on the back of the hand, or on the palm, or on one of the fingers.

"As soon as you notice any kind of reaction, any kind of movement, or any kind of feeling in either hand, place your attention upon that hand and upon the area where you felt the reaction and forget about the other hand completely.

"There, I just noticed a little movement in the little finger of your right hand. Place your attention upon that finger. See if you can figure out what caused that finger to move and see if you can anticipate what's going to happen next. Can you guess which finger is going to move next? Will it be the forefinger or the middle finger, or the ring finger or the thumb? Will it be something else rather than a movement? Will it be a feeling? Will it be a sensation? Your hand might become light and might develop a cool feeling. With many subjects that is what is reported. Some subjects report that the palm of the hand starts to arch and with others the fingers start to move and tremble in a strange way. All the while in most subjects the hand becomes lighter and cooler and after a while one finger lifts up off the thigh, then another, then a third, and finally, the whole hand tends to lift up off the thigh and seems to float into the air. Will this also happen with you? If so, how will it work? Will the fingers go up off your thigh first? Or will the wrist leave your thigh first, or the palm of the hand? Will the hand go up straight or will the hand cup or arch as it goes up? There, another finger just moved! Your forefinger this time. Yes, and your thumb has just lifted up off your thigh. It seems now that your hand is becoming lighter; I can see light now under your hand as it arches. By this time, it probably feels to you that it is barely resting upon your thigh, whereas the other hand, the left hand, is resting upon your thigh very heavily. But your right hand is getting lighter and lighter apparently. You can see it getting lighter. You can feel it getting lighter because you can actually see it lifting up off your thigh. Now, only two of tour fingers are touching your thigh. There they go, they're lifting up also and you may develop a strange feeling, as many subjects do, a strange sensation as if your arm and hand have a mind their own, as if they have a will and a motive power of their own which seem to cause it to float up into the air, to lift up higher and higher. As your hand continues to lift, keep watching it. Keep analyzing it. Keep trying to guess what's going to happen next. Will your hand lift straight up into the air or will it move outwards or inwards Laterally towards your body? Will the elbow bend or will your arm go up straight? In your case it seems like the arm is continuing straight up into the air and now your elbow seems to be lifting up off your thigh as well. Your arm is sort of stretching out and as you watch it you may be amazed to see these things happening apparently of their own accord. And all the while you keep on wondering what is going to happen next. Will the arm continue to lift up the way it is until it reaches shoulder level? This is what usually happens. Very often when the arm reaches shoulder level, the elbow begins to bend and the hand starts to float towards the face. Yes, it seems that's what is happening with you too. With some subjects of course, other reactions occur. With you, the hand is now apparently approaching your face. Slowly but steadily, it seems to be moving closer and closer to your face.

"Now as your hand moves closer and closer to your face, it actually indicates your readiness to go into hypnosis. In fact, you are going into hypnosis with a speed and readiness dictated by your subconscious mind. When you are inwardly ready, when your subconscious mind is ready for you to drop into hypnosis, your hand will touch your face. That will be a signal denoting your inner readiness to go into hypnosis. As soon as your hand touches your face, therefore, your eyes will close and you will drop into a deep, sound, hypnotic sleep. Your hand is moving ever closer, closer, and closer. It is now only a couple of inches from your face. At this point you might try to guess which part of your hand will touch which part of your face. Will the thumb touch your nose? Will the back of your hand touch your chin or your forehead? Frankly, it doesn't matter which part of the hand touches which part of the face. As soon as there's a contact, your eyes at that point will close because you will be ready to go into hypnosis and you will indeed drop into a deep, hypnotic sleep. It's coming closer and closer; your hand is almost touching now. Your thumb is almost touching your nose. There it goes, it has touched; your eyes are closed, and you are dropping into a deep, hypnotic sleep! So let yourself go completely and go down, way down, way down deep into a restful hypnotic state."

At this point you assume control, and if you wish, you can deepen the hypnosis with the standard method before you actually begin to work.

The foregoing method is an example of a Permissive Induction Technique. As you noticed, at the beginning no direct statements were made. A number of possibilities were brought forward to the subject indicating what had happened with other subjects. The subject before you then picks one of these alternatives, whatever it may be; and as you begin to see something occurring, as a visible reaction occurs, you point it out to the subject and he feels that it is happening of its own accord, not that you have caused it to happen. In this way you lead him gradually along until he goes into hypnosis. At the end of the method, of course, it is advisable to become somewhat more firm and emphatic and authoritarian in order to assume hypnotic control and to establish rapport.

VARIATIONS OF RESPONSES AND TECHNIQUE

With some subjects, the hand may go up a few inches and not continue to move any further. If four or five minutes have elapsed and the hand hasn't moved, it is usually advisable to change your tactics somewhat. You therefore proceed in this fashion:

"Your hand has now gone up about 4 inches. That is sufficient. Now I am going to count back from ten to one. As I count back from ten to one, your arm will gradually retrace its course; gradually drop back upon your thigh. When your hand drops back upon your thigh at the count of one, your eyes will close and you will drop deep into hypnosis. Ten!—your arm is starting to go down now. Nine!—it is slowly retracing its course. Eight!—going down, down. Seven!—and as your hand goes down, you go down, deeper and deeper into hypnosis. Six!—the closer and closer your hand goes down towards your thigh, the closer

51

and closer you come to a deep, sound, hypnotic state. Five!—coming down, down, and you're going down, deeper and deeper. Four!—relaxing more completely. Three!—your hand is dropping to your thigh. Two!—right down upon your thigh. One!—your eyes are closed now and you're going deeper into hypnosis. Deep, sound and restful hypnotic state."

Arm levitation occurs readily in those subjects who are capable of sensorimotor activity. This is usually indicated by a positive response to the Arms Rising and Falling test. With other subjects who do not react readily the arm levitation method of induction may not work in the sense that you may not be able to elicit any levitation responses.

However, it would not be wise to stop in the middle of the method with the admission of failure. The wiser procedure is to switch to a different method. The switch can be accomplished in a casual way so that the subject will riot even know that one method has been abandoned and another one substituted. Since you have not been saying anything really definite to the subject, since you have not said unequivocally that the arm would rise but only that many subjects report that such action occurs, you would therefore logically be able to switch around to another method by proceeding in this fashion:

"With most subjects the hand gets lighter and eventually rises up. However, with some subjects, rather than getting lighter, the hands and arms seem to become heavier. Possibly this is the reaction that you are now feeling. Perhaps you feel now the weight of your hands upon your thighs. Perhaps you feel the warmth of your hands through the cloth of your trousers (or your dress). As you continue to feel this weight and you continue to feel this warmth, your arms and hands seem to be becoming heavier and heavier and they seem to be almost digging into your thighs, making indentations in your thighs.

"As your arms become heavier and heavier, you notice a heaviness developing in your eyelids. Your eyes are barely open now; in fact it's becoming difficult to keep your eyes open. As your hands and arms become heavier and heavier, your eyelids become heavier and heavier. You feel like closing your eyes. Soon you may indeed close them. I will now count from one to ten. On the count often your eyes will close and you'll go deep into hypnosis."

What you are actually doing here is calling attention to the natural heaviness of the arms, a fact that is more likely to be in evidence because of gravity. Then you associate the heaviness of the arms with the heaviness of the eyelids. Actually, you are shifting to a standard method of induction in which gazing at the hands becomes tantamount to looking at a fixation object. Then you associate more and more with the heaviness of the lids and the eyes and you go into suggestions of drowsiness and sleepiness and gradually lead the person on into one of the standard methods. You can actually switch to the Intermittent Counting and Suggestion method, so that the counting to ten, interrupted by suggestions, becomes your new procedure. You can also, if you desire, switch to Progressive Relaxation and proceed as with the standard technique.

CONFUSION AND DISTRACTION METHODS

In a sense, the Arm and Hand Levitation method is based somewhat on distracting the subject from what the operator is saying. Therefore, by becoming aware of movements of his own body, he does not listen too closely to the operator and therefore the suggestions of going into hypnosis tend to go more readily into the subconscious. The methods that follow are more closely based on distraction and confusion. It is more obvious with these methods that the operator is attempting to get the subject not to listen to him too closely. These methods are a far cry from the old idea that the subject must concentrate hard on what the operator is saying and must make his mind a blank to everything except the operator's voice. The following is a rather effective confusion technique based on the Arm and Hand Levitation method:

You start as with the Arm Levitation method and you keep on until the hand has risen slightly off the thigh. Then you tell the subject to start counting backwards from 100, aloud. He starts counting backwards; while doing so he has to watch his hand, of course; he has to keep his conscious mind on his counting, and he also *thinks* that he has to listen to you. Therefore he is doing three things at the same time. Since the fact that his arm has risen slightly indicates that he is already partly in hypnosis, he finds it difficult to do three things at the same time. He becomes confused. His counting shows it. He may skip a number or repeat a number, or he may start going up instead of down. As his confusion increases, the operator becomes somewhat Louder, a bit more insistent, contributing further to the confusion.

Somewhere along the line, perhaps when the subject reaches 60 or 50 or 40, his confusion becomes so great that his annoyance is obvious. His brow may crease up, his voice may indicate annoyance, and he may show every indication of being extremely irritated and confused. Therefore, at the psychological moment—at the peak of the confusion—the operator suddenly drops what he is doing and commandingly and insistently says, "Close your eyes! Stop your counting; drop your hand and go into a deep sound sleep!"

The subject responds very readily because he is glad to be relieved of the confusing situation. In a sense, therefore, he seeks relief by retreating into hypnosis. The confusion method affords the subject an escape from an intolerable situation and he often drops readily into hypnosis and sometimes more deeply than he had done in previous attempts.

Sometimes, when a subject is doing too well, and is not becoming sufficiently confused, it may be advisable for the operator to go into the Intermittent Counting and Suggestion method. That is, he may start to count up from one, telling the subject he will go deeper on each count. Therefore, we have a situation where the subject is counting backward and the operator is counting forward, sort of "against the grain." This contributes greatly to the subject's confusion.

The following method embodies confusion, distraction, and visualization. I have found this method to be excellent for group induction. It is far superior to the Progressive Relaxation method. I shall give it here in some detail. You prepare the subject as you would for Progressive Relaxation and proceed as follows:

"As you sit there with your eyes closed, listen easily and effortlessly to my voice. In fact, you don't really have to listen to me. If I had my way, I would not have you. Listening to me at all—consciously, that is. You see, whether you are listening to me consciously or not your subconscious mind is getting everything that I'm saying. Your conscious mind tends to be somewhat of a hindrance, so if I could arrange it, I would have you not listening to me at all. I therefore have a suggestion, which will help you to accomplish this difficult task.

"I will give you something to do which will occupy your conscious mind. Thus you will be less likely to listen to me closely. I would like you to visualize—imagine—that you are looking up into a night sky. You may see a cloudy sky, or you may see a clear, deep blue sky with stars twinkling in it. Frankly, it doesn't matter what kind of a sky you see. Whatever comes to your mind, that is satisfactory.

"Now imagine that you see a wheel up in the sky. It's an incongruous situation, but nevertheless imagine you see some sort of a wheel directly above you against the background of the night sky. You may see a wagon wheel, or it might be a spinning wheel, or it could be a bicycle wheel—perhaps even a casino roulette wheel. Whatever kind of a wheel occurs to you, whatever kind of a wheel you see in your mind, look at it, watch it, and as you do, you will notice that it gradually starts to recede, gradually starts to go up into the sky. As it does so, it may remain in a stationary position, or it may be revolving, slowly or rapidly. Whatever the wheel does in your mind, let it do it. Don't try to force it to do anything in any way.

"Gradually, you will notice that as the wheel recedes into the heavens, it becomes smaller and smaller. Eventually, after five, or possibly ten or fifteen minutes, it will disappear behind the clouds or perhaps mix with the stars and disappear in that way.

"As you keep visualizing the wheel against the background of the sky, I want you now to do something else. Mentally, I want you to start to count back from 100 at about this speed (and you illustrate the count, going at about 2 second intervals). As you are counting backwards mentally and watching the wheel up in the sky, your mind will be occupied with this task and you will therefore be less likely to listen to me. That is exactly what I want to accomplish. As your conscious mind is occupied with the two tasks that I have given you, your subconscious will be free to accept the suggestions that I make and therefore you will go very readily and deeply into hypnosis.

"Now as you watch the wheel receding into the sky, and as you keep counting backwards, you find yourself relaxing more and more." Keep on in this vein; doing either a Progressive Relaxation or some other method that can be done with the eyes closed. Because the subject is not listening to you too closely, the subconscious mind is more easily accessible and he goes readily into hypnosis. As you go on this way, you keep throwing in occasional suggestions that when he reaches the count of one, he will raise his right forefinger slightly to indicate that he has completed his task. Just throw this suggestion in occasionally. It gets into his subconscious too, and when he reaches the count of one, his right forefinger goes up, often spontaneously. Whether it goes up spontaneously or whether he voluntarily raises it, you assume at that point, that he's in hypnosis and you become somewhat move authoritarian and take over.

You then proceed with the usual tests and with whatever deepening measure you want to take.

I have found the Distraction method very helpful with those subjects who have been under the misconception that they have to listen very closely to what the operator is saying. In doing so, they actually defeat their own purpose because the effort of listening is a conscious effort. The conscious effort of the mind tends to prevent the dissociation of the conscious from the subconscious and Lends to prevent hypnosis. Over-anxiety on the part of the subject has a similar frustrating effect.

REHEARSAL TECHNIQUE

The Rehearsal Technique is used only as a last resort. It is time consuming and therefore would only be feasible when every other method has failed.

You take the subject into your confidence and you tell him in effect the following:

"Now look here, I have used every method that I know. You have failed to respond. I know one more method which I am quite certain will work—if you agree to submit to it. In this method you have to agree to devote another ten or twelve separate sessions. All I want you to do is pretend that you are going into hypnosis. Act the part of the hypnotized subject. Pretend that you are conforming to the experiments I am giving you. Pretend that everything is working. Make believe that you are an actor in a play, playing the role of a hypnotized subject. At no time are you to test yourself to see whether you actually are in hypnosis. Just play a part."

If the subject agrees to do this, you proceed with any method of induction. He pretends to go into hypnosis. Then you do the Eye Catalepsy Test. He pretends he can't open his eyes. You do the Arm Catalepsy Test. He pretends he can't put him arm down. You continue with other similar tests, especially those that have to do with muscular inability. You avoid amnesia tests, anesthesia tests, and hallucination experiments.

After three or four sessions, the subject begins to wonder whether he actually could lower his arm or whether he actually could open his eyes, *if he indeed did try*. When a person pretends to have an inability to lower his arm, he doesn't actually know whether he could or not unless he did make an effort. Since he must not really lower it—since he is only pretending—it leaves a doubt in his mind. Session after session, the doubt increases. In the meantime, you are able to get indications from his subjective responses of the progress that you are making. After awakening from hypnosis, he may indicate that he had feelings of numbness, or a tingling sensation in the fingertips. He may indicate that he had feelings of heaviness, or feelings of lightness or floating. He may, upon awakening, develop time distortion; that is, he may have a distorted conception of how long he was in hypnosis. This is a very good sign. Therefore, after ten or twelve sessions, if you have achieved some of these subjective indications and you have fairly good reason to believe that your subject may indeed be in hypnosis, you finally try a crucial test.

Perhaps in the middle of a catalepsy test, you suddenly say—"Now, I want you to *actually* try to lower your arm; but you cannot do it! Really try to put it down! But you cannot lower it! Your arm is stuck, cataleptic, and you cannot lower it! Now, go deep into hypnosis!"

This very often works. The idea behind it is similar to the idea of a person lying constantly about the same thing. After a while, he is not sure whether he is telling the truth or lying. So whether you actually carry out a certain act or only pretend to carry it out, it causes similar patterns to develop in the brain. The act becomes a reality.

AN EXCELLENT VISUALIZATION— DIS TRACTION METHOD

This method can be done both individually and with groups. Preparing the subject as for the Progressive Relaxation Method, you proceed as follows:

"I want you to visualize, with your eyes closed, that you have a blackboard before you. If you have a good imagination, you can actually see the blackboard. If you cannot see it, simply imagine you do. Now imagine that in the center of the blackboard there has been drawn a large circle, possibly twelve or fourteen inches in diameter. The circle is drawn in chalk. Inside the circle there is a large X drawn in such a way that the four feet of the X touch the circle at four different points. Now, I want you to imagine that you're picking up the eraser. It is your job to erase the X without damaging the circle. Since the X in touching the circle at four points, this may not be a very easy thing to do. Therefore, I make the following suggestion. Using a corner of the eraser, simply make a little break in each leg of the X, just below where it touches the circle. Proceed to make it now in one leg—in the third—and in the fourth, very carefully. With that accomplished, you can now proceed to erase the rest of the X without damaging the circle. Now switch the eraser around to the other hand and pick up a piece of chalk. Draw a capital A inside the circle, but make the A only about half the size of the circle to be sure that you don't damage the circle; that's important. Now that you have made an A, with the eraser in the other hand, erase the A. Now make a B, and with the eraser, erase the B.

Now make a C, and now erase the C. Now hold everything for a moment and listen to my further instructions. I'm going to give you a signal in a moment, at which point you will continue making the next letter and erasing it, and go right on down through the alphabet until you have made and erased the letter Z. I want you to keep your attention on what you are doing and don't make any special effort to listen to me. With your conscious mind thus occupied, my hypnotic suggestions will go directly into your subconscious and produce a deep, hypnotic state. When you have completed the alphabet, I want you to put the eraser down, put the chalk down, and just raise your right forefinger about half an inch, to indicate to me that you have completed your job. At that point you will be in deep hypnosis.

"Now, make the next letter, the letter D and erase it and keep right on going, paying no further attention to me. You are becoming very, very relaxed now—very drowsy, sleepy. Your entire body is becoming completely relaxed. Every time you make a letter and erase it, you go deeper into hypnosis." And continue in this vein until the person raises his forefinger; then assume control in the usual fashion.

FOURTEEN
INSTANTANEOUS METHODS, INDIRECT METHODS and WAKING HYPNOSIS

INSTANTANEOUS METHODS

Those methods, which produce hypnosis instantly or almost instantly, are called Instantaneous Methods. My book, *Techniques of Speed Hypnosis,* deals comprehensively with the rapid methods of induction. For our purpose in this book, it should suffice to explain the principles on which these methods are based and to give a few examples. Actually there are only two instantaneous methods, or putting it differently, two types of rapid techniques.

1. The first type is based on post-hypnotic suggestion. A subject who goes into at least the third stage is given a signal by means of which he can be instantaneously projected into hypnosis thereafter. This ability of going into hypnosis at a signal becomes permanent with sufficient repetition.

The signal can be almost anything. It can be a word, counting to five or to ten, taking a few deep breaths, or any other signal that is agreed upon during hypnosis. The operator gives the subject the instructions in a very precise manner and the subject carries these instructions out in the subsequent waking state, upon being exposed to the signal agreed upon.

Actually, when this has been repeated a few times, the subject becomes convinced of his ability to go into hypnosis instantly whereupon this ability becomes a perm-anent one. Therefore, the signal is not actually required. The subject's acceptance that he can go back into hypnosis instantly is sufficient.

2. Even without being previously hypnotized, some subjects can be rapidly projected into hypnosis. These methods do require a good subject. Among the American population, only about 25% are capable of going into rapid hypnosis without having been previously hypnotized.

The usual method is to produce in the subject a *conviction* that something unusual is occurring. Thereupon, a sudden command of "Sleep!" drives him into hypnosis.

The Hand-Clasp Test is a good example. The subject is told to clasp his hands together and that upon the count of three he will be unable to open them. Then while he is struggling to open his hands, and he is convinced that he cannot do so, the sudden command of "Sleep!" at this point drops him into the hypnotic state.

Actually, the mere fact that he could not open his hands is evidence that he is already in a fleeting, waking hypnotic trance. The command of going to sleep is tantamount to a declaration that a hypnotic state now exists.

All the other methods of induction of rapid hypnosis given in the book, *Techniques of Speed Hypnosis*, are based on the same principle: a conviction that something unusual is occurring is forced upon the subject. A command to go into hypnosis does the rest. Once the operator Linderstands this principle thoroughly, he does not actually need to use a definite method. He can invent his own variations.

INDIRECT OR DISGUISED TECHNIQUES

Hypnosis may be induced in a disguised fashion so that the subject does not know he is being hypnotized. It must be stressed that this is not to imply that the subject is being hypnotized against his will. The approach is made in such a way that he is actually guided into hypnosis without being aware that the condition that he is in is hypnosis.

The success of indirect methods of induction depends upon the subject's misconception about hypnosis. The average person thinks that to be hypnotized, he has to be unconscious or asleep. Since unconsciousness and sleep have nothing to do with hypnosis, he can therefore be readily guided into a hypnotic state without being aware of the fact.

THREE APPROACHES TO INDIRECT INDUCTIONS

1. The first type is through Progressive Relaxation. This method is explained thoroughly in my booklet, "The Best and Easiest Disguised Methods of Inducing Hypnosis." The procedure is the same as when doing the Progressive Relaxation Test. However, the words "hypnosis," "sleepy," "drowsy," "sleep" are not employed. The subject thinks he is only being relaxed. When the relaxation technique is over, he is in hypnosis. If he has eye catalepsy, it is evidence that he already is in a hypnotic state—although he may not be aware of the fact.

2. The second approach to indirect induction is through the sensorimotor reactions of the subject. To explain this type of method, I can advantageously cite an actual case that occurred several years ago.

A woman phoned me to arrange hypnotic conditioning for childbirth. During the telephone conversation, I discovered that she had only two more weeks to go before the expected delivery. I explained to her that wasn't sufficient time for the conditioning. I explained that ordinarily we start in the fourth or fifth month and that quite a few things have to be done to prepare the expectant mother for a hypnotic delivery. I suggested, therefore, that she forget about it for this pregnancy but call me for the next one. She was extremely disappointed, but since there was nothing else to do, we terminated our conversation.

The next year she called me again.

"What!" I said in surprise. "Are you pregnant again?"

"No," she replied, "but I want to be ready this time."

She came over with her husband and the first question she asked me was:

"Mr. Arons, do you think you could really hypnotize me?"

I asked her why she was so doubtful. Whereupon she admitted to me that when I turned her down the previous year, she had gone to two other hypnotists. Each tried to hypnotize her on three different occasions. Both failed and both declared that she was impossible to hypnotize. She came to me, therefore, with this attitude of defeatism.

I explained that I could not possibly tell her for certain whether she could be hypnotized or not under the circumstances, but I was willing to test her and would then be able to give her a better idea. She agreed to be tested.

I knew at this point that I could not possibly succeed with her with the methods that the others had employed. She was so expectant of failure with these methods they could not possibly work. I therefore questioned her exhaustively in an effort to determine what they had done. For testing, both had used authoritarian tests. One had used the Falling Backwards Test and one had used the Hands Clasp rest. Both had used the Pendulum Test; this was the only thing that worked. For induction methods, they had used the Direct Stare, Progressive

Relaxation, and direct fixation techniques. None had an effect upon her. I asked her whether any of them had used the Arms Rising and Falling Test or the Sensor Motor Techniques. She was not familiar with the terms. Now I had an idea how to proceed.

"I have one more test, which, if you pass, will indicate quite clearly that you can be hypnotized. Please sit down in the chair. Place your hands upon your thighs and I will now test your sensorimotor reactions."

"As you sit there I want you to look down at your hands and listen easily and effortlessly to my voice. As you observe your hands, you will notice certain peculiar reactions in your body. You may feel your breathing, you may feel the pulsing of the blood in your veins and you may feel other reactions, which are termed sensorimotor responses. As you look at your hands, you may notice little movements—perhaps a twitch of the fingers. Perhaps you may notice inner sensations like a tug of a ligament, a twinge of a nerve. I want you to observe carefully any physical response or any feeling that you may have. Analyze each movement. Analyze every sensation."

The reader will notice that I had started the Arm and [land Levitation method of induction. I used it, however, as a test and I deliberately told the subject to "analyze," to watch, knowing full well that the average subject would be distracted from the mere idea of hypnosis when such words as "analyze" were employed.

As the subject watched her hands, the movements started almost immediately. She had very good hand levitation reactions. As soon as I saw something happening, I pointed these reactions out to her and kept urging her to analyze whatever she saw, to try to figure out exactly what was happening. Depending upon these suggestions to keep her off the track that she was actually being hypnotized.

Her arm rose steadily and then, upon indirect suggestion, the elbow started to bend and the hand started to approach the face. I kept on in the same vein until finally her hand touched her face—at which point I suggested that she would be much more comfortable if she would allow her eyes to close, and rather than looking at her hand, would feel it against her face. I suggested that she feel the touch of her hand, the warmth of her hand; I told her to think about whatever other feeling she might have. Her hand remained in that position. I kept on for about four or five minutes just to be sure. With the hand in that upraised position, the average subject would have become extremely fatigued and would have allowed the hand to drop or at least to sag. There was no such sign with this subject. This was a clear indication to me that she was already in hypnosis. However I could not let her know that this was the case.

My problem now was how to test her without giving away that she was being hypnotized. I therefore proceeded as follows:

"As your hand rests against your face, that position has caused the blood to run out of your arm and into your body causing a certain numbness to develop in your hand due to the lack of blood. This numbness is becoming more and more profound as your hand remains in the air so that the back of your hand feels especially numb, feels almost as if it has been anesthetized. Although you may feel a touch on your hand, you can feel no pain in it because there isn't sufficient blood there to give you the proper sensations." As I spoke I started to pinch the skin on the back of her hand and I watched her face intently. There was no reaction. I pinched harder. Still there was no reaction. Finally I said to her:

"Tell me, can you feel anything?"

"Sure," she replied. "You're touching me."

I then called to her husband and motioned to him to pinch his wife's hand. He proceeded very gingerly at first, but when he saw she was not reacting, he pinched harder and harder. Again I asked her if she felt anything.

"Of course," she replied. "Jack is touching me."

This was enough for me. I then said to her, "On the count of five you will open your eyes." I did not mention anything about awakening. I then counted from one to five and she opened her eyes and said:

"Well, what do you think?"

When I declared that she had been in hypnosis, she just would not believe it. She would never have believed that she had been pinched, had her husband not been present. Even so, it took quite a little convincing for her to finally accept the fact that she had anesthesia in her hand. In other words, she was already somewhere between the third and the fourth stage.

The above is an excellent illustration of the disguised sensorimotor approach to hypnosis.

3. The third approach to indirect induction is through the use of placebos. A placebo, in medical parlance, is an innocuous drug or pill which is purported to produce a certain effect, but has no actual value. Placebos can be made of sugar, bread, or saline injections. Placebos of this type should be used only medically.

A physician may give a subject a placebo with a suggestion that if the subject takes this with a glass of water, he will be fast asleep in two minutes. With the proper subject, this works amazingly well.

Following is a placebo method that I observed many years ago in a dentist's office.

The dentist told an eleven-year-old boy who was an extremely troublesome patient that he had obtained a "special nitrous oxide" which, he said, would not put him to sleep, but would only place him in a dreamy state in which he would be completely insensible to pain and would be able to very easily tolerate the drilling. He then placed the nitrous oxide mask over the subject's nose and mouth, told him to breathe deeply and to count back from ten to one. By the time the boy reached seven, he was "out." His body became limp, he relaxed completely, and the dentist proceeded to work. The boy was aware of things around him, he was able to answer the dentist's questions; he was in a peculiar, dreamy, detached condition, and he felt absolutely no pain or discomfort from the dental work.

Actually, the nitrous oxide mask was not even connected to the machine. The machine had been turned on so that it emitted a peculiar buzz, but this was merely for effect.

In a sense, hypno-discs and similar hypno-aids are placebos. The passes, with or without contact, which the hypnotist sometimes makes over the subject's face and body, are likewise placebo applications. The placebo has a purely suggestive effect.

As pointed out earlier, the indirect methods are effective because the average subject thinks that, to be hypnotized, he must lapse into unconsciousness or into sleep. Since hypnosis is not related to either, he goes into it without being aware that he is in hypnosis.

WAKING HYPNOSIS

In order to present waking hypnosis clearly to the reader, I feel it is advisable to present a theory of my own. I do not present this theory as "the last word." It is merely something that, it seems to me, helps to understand the phenomenon of hypnosis.

To my mind, the hypnotic "trance" is a misnomer. It is not a sleep state. It is not an unconscious state. Actually, it does not differ appreciably from the waking state.

The hypnotic "trance," as we observe it, seems to be something that the subject has learned to "act out." The subject, in some way, predetermines how a person behaves and how he looks when hypnotized, and then proceeds to play the part.

I do not mean to imply that the subject is faking. He assumes the pose that he feels is required in the hypnotic state. He does it all on an unconscious level. He lives the part. It is real to him. A subject who is capable of somnambulism will therefore feel that he is either "asleep" and "unconscious," or anything else that he is led to believe that he should feel, especially if the suggestions that he receives are in line with what he previously anticipated from hypnosis.

Nevertheless, there is ample evidence that a potential somnambule can accomplish in the waking state exactly the same things that he can accomplish in hypnosis. The subject who does not go into somnambulism, who is only able to achieve a light state, is often disappointed that he doesn't fall asleep or that he does not go unconscious as he had previously expected to do. He doesn't feel hypnotized at all and is very often surprised when he can't open his eyes or lower his arm, as is suggested by the operator. He has to be reeducated in order to avoid his rejecting the phenomena that he is experiencing. Some subjects will experience the phenomena of light and medium hypnosis and yet reject this as being hypnosis because it is not consistent with what they had expected. Rejecting the hypnosis may also cause them to fail to gain the benefit From suggestion that they would otherwise achieve.

TWO AVENUES TO WAKING HYPNOSIS

There are two ways of demonstrating waking hypnosis; two avenues leading towards the performance of waking hypnosis experiments.

One of these is through post-hypnotic suggestion. This is the simpler method. With a person in hypnosis, you simply tell him that after he awakens, although he is wide-awake in every respect, he will still do exactly what he is told. Then you wake him up, and make simple suggestions that are within the scope of his level of hypnosis. For example, you can tell him that he can't raise his foot from the floor, and he cannot do it. You can tell him that he can't separate his hands, and he cannot do it. If he has achieved analgesia in the hypnotic state, you can tell him that his arm or any part of his body is now analgesic, and so it will become. The fact that he was previously hypnotized makes it easier for him to accept these waking suggestions, and therefore they work.

The second way is by extending the suggestibility tests. That is, you start with the simpler tests, like the Arm Rising and Falling Test. When that works, you proceed to the Falling Backward Test; when that succeeds you go on to the Hands-Clasp Test. And here is where you should begin to see my point.

If a person is unable to separate his hands in the waking state, actually he is already in hypnosis. In fact, he is in the second stage of hypnosis because here you are controlling isolated muscle groups—the groups of muscles on his arms. Therefore, you can simply assume that he is capable of performing experiments of the second-stage Level without even being hypnotized.

Try it. After having done the Hands-Clasp Test, have your subject raise his arm and tell him that it is cataleptic and that he cannot lower it and cannot bend it. Do it rather forcefully. Keep his attention fixed by having him gaze at his thumbnail or your eyes and, you will see, he will not be able to bend or lower his arm, providing he has a fair degree of acceptance of this fact. Some subjects require an actual hypnotic trance to be able to do these things because they have a low degree of acceptance. They just don't believe that without being hypnotized they can do these things. If they do believe, if they have acceptance, they can indeed respond as suggested.

Go on further. Tell him now that he will count and will be unable to say a certain number—if his capacity for hypnosis is of sufficient depth, he will have a number block. You can carry him even further. Tell him that he has analgesia, and that he can't feel any pain. Again, if he is in a sufficient level, that will occur—without the need to put him into trance.

In other words, you can lead him along, step by step, from a simple experiment to a more complicated one and continue to the limit of his capacity as a hypnotic subject. All this can be done without putting him into any kind of hypnotic state to begin with. It must again be stressed that all this will be accomplished providing he has acceptance.

Instantaneous hypnosis, indirect hypnosis and waking hypnosis are all part and parcel of this same phenomenon of acceptance of suggestion. The trance is actually not necessary. The trance is like a conditioned reflex. It is something that the subject has learned to anticipate and goes into, or achieves, when he "goes into hypnosis."

Understanding these things will enable you to understand the phenomenon of suggestibility in everyday life.

The ability to accept suggestion seems to depend upon the subject's ability to keep his mind on a certain train of thought to the general exclusion of other thoughts. The mind is apparently capable of thinking of several things at the same time, but the subject has to be able to keep his mind almost exclusively on a special train of thought and to allow other thoughts to flit through or glance off without seriously registering upon it. That is why suggestibility varies so much.

LESSON FIFTEEN
EIGHT BEST TECHNIQUES FOR DEEPENING HYPNOSIS

The problem of deepening the hypnotic state to the maximum degree possible for a given subject is a more serious one than the problem of inducing the trance in the first instance. It is common knowledge that at least 90% of the American population can be hypnotized at the first attempt or after a number of induction sessions. It is known, too (though many of us are reluctant to accept the fact), that only a small percentage of the hypnotizable are able to reach the somnambulistic stage. Induction methods and related information can be found in abundance in most books and courses on the subject of hypnotism, but procedures for deepening the trance have received but sketchy treatment in most published works. Stage performers are not greatly concerned with the problem because, having large audiences for subject selection, they rarely fail to isolate a number of somnambules for demonstration purposes. It is the hypnotist working in a private office setting, faced with the task of producing results in any subject who presents himself, who is seriously affected.

Professional hypnotherapists have resorted to the rationalization that even light degrees of trance are sufficient for therapeutic purposes. This may indeed be so; they use hypnoidal states, reverie, relaxation, waking suggestion and other means for conveying therapeutic suggestion to their patients. For some purposes, however, the lighter stages are inadequate. Some psychotherapists claim that a majority of subjects will ultimately attain a deep trance, providing the hypnotist has enough skill and patience, and providing still further, I might add, that the subject has sufficient time and money to test the operator's skill and patience.

I have found in my experience that practical considerations require that a subject be projected into a workable degree of hypnosis in six to ten sessions. I have found further that the average subject can reach the maximum degree possible for him within that time. It is usually a waste of time, money and energy to expect a subject to exceed the depth of his tenth hypnosis. It is hoped that the information in the following pages will help the frustrated hypnotist to deepen the hypnotic trance of his subjects as much as possible within a reasonable time—and to make the best of the situation with those who remain on a superficial level. It is a practical assumption that subjects who reach a certain degree after ten sessions will, with but a few exceptions, remain at that level.

EIGHT TYPES OF DEEPENING TECHNIQUES
Deepening techniques can arbitrarily be divided into eight general headings:
1. Deepening by Realization
2. Deepening by Pyramiding of Suggestion
3. Deepening by Post-hypnotic Suggestion
4. Deepening by Repeated Induction
5. Deepening by Placebo Suggestion
6. Deepening through Sensorimotor Reactions
7. Feed-back Methods
8. Counting Methods

I. Deepening by Realization

In most instances of initial induction the subject does not know that he is under hypnosis, since he hears the operator, is more or less aware of his surroundings and does not *feel different* from the way he usually feels. He does not feel that he is *asleep* or in a *trance*, as many subjects have previously conceived that they would feel. It is therefore necessary to make him *realize* that he is indeed hypnotized. One of the most elementary of the realization suggestions is to challenge him to open his eyes, at the same time stating convincingly that he is powerless to do so. His inability to perform this simple function often startles him into the realization that he is not as *awake* as he thought. Any of the muscular control experiments can be used for this purpose; an arm can be made rigid, for example, and the subject challenged to bend or lower it, with patter somewhat as follows:

"Your arm is outstretched before you, stiff and rigid like a bar of steel. You are completely powerless to bend or lower it. In fact the harder you try—the more impossible it is, because you are in hypnosis, you see, and are implicitly obedient to my every command. What's even more remarkable, you will notice that as you try to lower your arm, it begins to go up instead! The harder you try to lower your arm—the higher and higher it goes. Now try, try hard to bend your arm or put it down—and now you see it keeps rising higher and higher. You simply cannot lower your arm until I say that you can!" What you are doing here is impressing forcibly upon the subject's consciousness that he is indeed under your "hypnotic control"—else why can he not do something so simple as lowering his arm?

With some subjects realization suggestions are more effective in the post-hypnotic state. A suggestion may be made that a few minutes after awakening he would become aware of a terrible itching sensation in his back just between the shoulder blades, where it would be difficult to scratch.

"You will be very annoyed with this itching," you continue, "and will go into all sorts of contortions to scratch this spot, even rubbing your back against the wall and against articles of furniture. But nothing will help. Finally, you will appeal for my help in the matter, because only I will be able to relieve this itching. I will simply snap my fingers twice—like this (snap, snap) and the itching will disappear instantly. This will convince you beyond the shadow of a doubt that you are indeed under hypnosis, so that when I hypnotize you again you will go into a much deeper trance, much more quickly and easily."

In short, you are making the subject realize that, in spite of the fact that he feels awake, hypnotic suggestions are working and causing him to fall deeper into hypnosis.

2. Pyramiding of Suggestions

Pyramiding of suggestions is usually combined with the realization technique. Thus, no sooner has the subject realized that he cannot lower his arm than you say:

"Now, on the count of *three* your arm will go limp all at once and fall heavily to your side. And as it does so you will fall deeper and deeper asleep. One ... two ... three! There! Go deep asleep now—deeper asleep!"

Proceed immediately to other tests, while he is still amazed at the way the previous ones worked. Nothing succeeds like success. While the subject is still emotionally imbued with the confidence of his first success, pile on other suggestions, gradually increasing their complexity as one after the other is carried out. The idea is to follow up each successful culmination of a suggestion with the assertion that he is going deeper and deeper into hypnosis. And as it becomes apparent that the trance is becoming more profound, more advanced experiments are attempted. It is important to know how far to go, so that you stop just short of failure. Just as success increases a subject's confidence, so the realization of a failure can have a deleterious effect.

3. Post-hypnotic Suggestion

One of the better-known methods of deepening hypnosis is telling the subject just before awakening him that the next time he will go into a deeper trance much more quickly and easily. This suggestion is most effective when induction is repeated twice a week, but it has been found that it carries over from week to week. So common is this method that most hypnotists employ suggestion in this vein almost as a matter of course whether deepening is needed or not.

4. Repeated Induction

Continued rehypnotization is probably the most reliable way of deepening hypnosis. The mere procedure of reinducing the hypnotic state seems to have the effect of rendering it more profound, probably because, as the subject becomes accustomed to *letting go*, resistances of a conscious and unconscious nature fade away.

Ordinarily, this technique is coupled with post-hypnotic suggestion in bi-weekly, weekly, or daily sessions. However, rehypnotization during the same session is often helpful; sometimes a subject may be awakened and re-sensitized four or five times within a two-hour period, with five or ten minute intermissions to permit the operator to rest and to test the subject's post-hypnotic reactions.

The hypnotic sessions can be anywhere from fifteen to forty-five minutes in duration, most of the time being spent in repetition of suggestions. This method is hard work and requires persistence and stamina on the part of the operator. In recent years some shortcuts have been devised. These can be tried first to test their efficiency. Should results be unsatisfactory, the orthodox methods can be employed.

One of the shortcuts involves awakening a subject and rehypnotizing him immediately without giving him a chance to become fully aroused. I recommend the following procedure:

"I am going to awaken you," you tell the subject at the proper juncture. "At the count of *three* you will awaken and open your eyes. As you do so your eyes will meet mine as I stand over you. You will look intently into my eyes. I will then count slowly to *five*. As I count, you will very quickly become extremely sleepy. Your head will feel very heavy and your eyes will feel like closing. When I reach *three* your eyes will be half-closed and you will be almost asleep. When I reach *five* your eyes will close tightly, your head will droop and fall forward and you will go back into a deep, deep sleep. But deeper—much deeper than ever before—you'll go into a very deep, profound somnambulic sleep at the count of *five*. Now— one ... two ... three ... four ... five! Go deep asleep now—deeper, much deeper than ever before...."

I usually pass my open hand, without contact over the subject's face in the final count. Almost invariably, his eyes close as my fingers pass over them on the count of *five*. This procedure can be repeated four or five times in the same session with variations if desired. Ormond McGill, for instance, recommends awakening the subject, having him stand up, walk over to another chair, sit down, and then go to sleep with the counting routine, or perhaps at a certain signal as specified in the post-hypnotic suggestion. But the essence of the entire procedure is the repetition of the hypnotic induction in one form or another.

5. Deepening by Placebo Suggestion

In medical parlance a placebo is a pill, capsule, or injection of an innocuous substance, administered to the patient in the guise of medicine, in the hope that the accompanying suggestion will have the intended psychological effect. Wise doctors from time immemorial have used placebos, but today with the advancing knowledge of hypnotism and practical suggestion, placebo administration is enjoying a greater vogue than ever.

A placebo is merely an indirect hypnotic suggestion. Its use need not be restricted to medicine, though its application in therapy is most logical and feasible. In hypnotic work, it has limited application in cases where direct suggestion appears to meet subject resistance. The following example will give the reader some idea of how it may be employed.

I had hypnotized a patient in a dentist's office. The subject was in an intermediate stage, fluctuating between the mnesic and amnesic, with a good degree of analgesia but no anesthesia. Several extractions had been performed without great discomfort on previous occasions, but now the dentist was grinding a tooth down for a porcelain jacket and after fifteen minutes of grinding the analgesia was wearing thin. Ordinarily a supplementary chemical anesthetic would be used, but in this case I decided to try a placebo. I signaled my intention to the dentist, and then said:

"Doctor, the patient is in pain. Obviously, the hypnosis is not deep enough for all this grinding. I suggest you give him a small injection of that *new Procaine* that worked so well yesterday on Mr. B."

The doctor voiced his agreement and proceeded to prepare the injection. He went through all the motions of administering an injection, at the same time discussing the new drug with me, stressing that while it had the same analgesic effect as Novocain, it went to work more rapidly; also, the dentist always knew when the analgesia was complete because the patient would feel a strong tingling sensation in the fingertips. He actually punctured the gum in *pretending to make the injection.* Two minutes later the patient reported the awaited tingling and the dentist resumed his work without any further trouble. This strong, indirect suggestion of complete analgesia—actually, of course, nothing whatsoever was injected into the patient—had the effect of deepening the hypnotic state. Naturally, this type of suggestion must be handled very judiciously, and only with selected subjects.

Physicians and dentists are in the most fortunate position strategically to use placebo suggestions. Naturopaths use, instead of drugs, various appliances to which they attribute certain specific hypnotic effects; thus when only a light degree of hypnosis can be induced via ordinary methods, they may place the patient on a vibrating couch, Fit him with dark, multicolored goggles and have him gaze at blinking multi-colored lights, all of which are intended to, and often do, produce deeper hypnosis. Their manual adjustments, accompanied by suggestions of the specific results that were expected to follow, have similar effects on suitable patients. All these ruses, and others too numerous to mention, are in the nature of placebo suggestions. Even the so-called mesmeric passes with and without contact, which in the light of modern knowledge are used to serve the purpose of indirect suggestion, fall within the same category.

6. Deepening Through Sensorimotor Reactions

The Sensorimotor technique, more commonly known as the Arm and Hand Levitation method, is ordinarily employed in the induction procedure. When used for deepening purposes, suggestions of hand and arm levitation are commenced after a light degree of hypnosis has already been produced via a different method.

The premise behind this type of deepening technique is this:

Since, as is generally agreed, the subject remains in a light stage because of conscious or unconscious resistances within himself, it often helps to thrust the burden of the matter back upon himself The operator says, in effect:

"Now look here! You are in hypnosis, but for reasons beyond my control you refuse to go deeper. So now I leave it to you. You can go deeper if you really want to. We'll do hand and arm levitation now—your hand will rise off your thigh and your arm will continue rising, slowly but steadily, until it reaches shoulder level. Then your arm will bend at the elbow and your hand will approach your face. The speed of your reactions will be determined by your own subconscious willingness and desire to go into deep hypnosis. In other words— when you are ready to go into a deep trance—and not before—your hand will touch your Face. This will, in effect, be a signal from your subconscious mind that you are ready to go deep asleep. So as soon as your hand touches your face you will instantly, at that point, drop into a deep, sound, somnambulic sleep."

The levitation suggestions, ordinarily performed with the subject's eyes open and fixed on his hands, are in the case of deepening procedures done with the eyes closed; having the subject open his eyes while he is in a superficial trance would probably result in him becoming completely aroused. It must be understood that the sensorimotor reactions proceed at a pace which the subject himself sets. He goes into a deeper trance if and when he desires. At least that is the theory. If this does not work, the operator can easily disclaim responsibility for the subject's failure to go into a deep trance. The employment of this technique does require considerable skill; patience, too, will be found to be a helpful attribute of the operator.

7. Feed-Back Methods

In essence, the lightly hypnotized subject is taken on an imaginary walk through an endless, winding corridor or tunnel, or on a lazy canoe ride on a lake. During the course of these excursions into fantasy, the hypnotist conjures up various images and sensations, while the subject sits quietly in his chair; mentally experiencing whatever is suggested to him. He is not asked to perform any physical action or to speak; his reactions are investigated and evaluated post-hypnotically.

The subject is asked to imagine that he is lying comfortably in the canoe, which the operator is paddling, and that his hand is dragging in the water. It is suggested that the water is warm in one spot and cold in another. The appropriate sensations are described in detail. In the tunnel walk, a pail of ice-cold water is encountered and the subject is told to immerse his arm in it and to feel the sensation of freezing as they progress. Next, hallucinations of a verdant garden may be aroused and the subject is encouraged to enjoy the sight and smell of various flowers, fruits, etc. In other words, hallucinations of the senses are created; upon awakening the subject describes just how he felt, enabling the operator to determine which of the senses are more amenable to suggestion. Some subjects are able to hallucinate visual images easily, others are influenced by olfactory sensations, still others are susceptible to suggestions of tactile changes, etc. The idea, then, is to work on those senses which the individual subject shows to be most susceptible to suggestions. Thus, in subsequent hypnosis, pyramiding of suggestions is facilitated due to the avoidance of experiments that tend to fail. Often, deepening is accomplished during the canoe or tunnel trips, with the subject kept in a passive state through a number of successive inductions, progress being determined on the basis of post-hypnotic evaluations of each session. As had already been mentioned, combinations of several deepening techniques are advisable where indicated.

During the tunnel or corridor walk the subject is taken into rooms that appear in the side of the corridor. In these rooms, he is subjected to *crystal gazing*, theater fantasy, and other experiments that the operator may deem advisable. All these techniques are described in Wolberg's books in adequate detail. Readers who are not already familiar with them are urged to obtain a set of these books.

67

8. Deepening by Counting Backwards

One of the simplest and easiest deepening methods is counting backwards. It can be done in a variety of ways.

a. You simply tell the subject that you will now count backwards from one hundred and that on each count he will go deeper and deeper into hypnosis until at the count of one, he will be in the deepest hypnotic state possible for him at this time. Then all you do is count monotonously.

b. A variation of this is to count and, between each count, use the one word, "deeper." In other words, you say, "one-hundred—deeper," "ninety-nine— deeper," "ninety-eight—deeper," and so on until you have reached the count of "one."

c. Another variation is to have the subject count. It's usually best to have him count mentally, while you keep perfectly still. Instruct him that when he reaches the count of one, he will raise his right forefinger to show you that he is finished so that you can continue. While he is doing this, you can actually leave the room if you wish, keeping your eye on your watch and coming back within five or six minutes before he is actually finished.

d. Another variation yet is to have him count back-wards while you are talking. Strangely enough, this works quite well; since his mind is partly occupied with the counting back-wards, he is less likely to pay too much attention consciously to what you are saying and tends to go into hypnosis more readily.

LESSON SIXTEEN
PRACTICAL USES OF HYPNOSIS
NON-THERAPEUTIC APPLICATIONS
(CASE STUDIES)

FUNCTION OF THE HYPNOSIS TECHNICIAN

The applications of hypnosis in the healing arts are well known and need not be elaborated here. There are, however, applications in other fields that are not familiar to most people. Such applications include the use of hypnosis in advertising and selling, in business management, in education, in law enforcement, and in sports.

In the past, only two areas of application were recognized, namely, in the healing arts and in entertainment. Since the American Medical Association formally approved hypnosis as a medical and dental tool, however, its use as a form of entertainment has declined and its practical values in medicine and the allied arts have come to the forefront. When hypnosis is employed in such areas as business and selling, in education and in sports, it is applied more as an educational tool than a medical modality, and is not considered to be governed by the restrictions of medical practice. These are called non-therapeutic applications.

Since the establishment of the AAEH (Association to Advance Ethical Hypnosis) in 1955, the non-therapeutic applications of hypnosis have received considerable attention. In addition, the medical and dental uses of hypnosis in the hands of lay (non-medical) hypnotists have attained a certain amount of recognition. Such activities, naturally, must be carried out only under medical supervision. The Association, which includes members of all the professions as well as serious laymen, has set up a Code of Ethics and Standards which attempts to regulate the practice of hypnosis by its members. The lay members of the Association are referred to as *hypno-technicians* or *hypnosis consultants*. The main objective of the AAEH is to establish hypno-technicians as members of "the healing team" on a professional par with registered nurses, X-Ray technicians, physical therapists and others who operate in an adjunctive capacity and under medical supervision.

Several states have already recognized the function of hypno-technicians, at least in principle. The Boards of Medical Examiners of the states of New Jersey and Montana and the Attorneys General of those states have, upon specific questioning by AAEH members, interpreted the Medical Practice Acts of their respective states as permitting lay hypnotists to practice their art providing their clients were referred to them by licensed medical doctors and that they carry out the instructions of those doctors. In a few cities, namely Orlando and Indian River City, Florida, special city ordinances have been passed licensing "Ethical Hypnotists" to practice hypnosis under medical supervision. It is hoped that eventually the various states will establish regular licensing procedures for hypno-technicians who operate under the Code of Ethics and Standards of the Association to Advance Ethical Hypnosis.

The applications of hypnosis described in the Following pages are considered in the framework of the operations of ethical hypno-technicians. The actual modes of the employment of hypnosis in the various conditions mentioned, however, would be similar whether the operator is a hypno-technician, a dentist, a psychologist, an educator, or a law enforcement officer. It must be understood, of course, that professional people use hypnosis only within their own areas of competence, and that they employ hypno-technicians who limit their activities to the area of competence of the referring or supervising doctor.

The applications which follow are presented in the form of case studies. For greater clarity, the studies are somewhat simplified, and in a few instances two or more cases are combined in order to illustrate the essential elements of each. The cases described are those that occur most frequently in the work of a hypno-technician.

HYPNOTIC ENFORCEMENT OF DIET

Case of G.S. Referred by her physician, Mrs. S. gave the usual account of having tried everything medical without success except for brief periods. Pills would work while she used them, but her weight increased again as soon as she stopped the medication. Strict diets would help her lose ten to fifteen pounds, but the effort involved was so fatiguing that invariably she put the weight back on again.

Mrs. S. was a light subject who was disappointed that she could not go into somnambulism. However, she started to lose weight after the second session and, with the help of self-hypnosis, lost 42 pounds in three months. Following is a sampling of the suggestions she received:

"Hereafter, you will find it *easier* and *easier* every day to stick to your doctor's diet. You will get more *filling satisfaction* from less food every day. You will eat and *enjoy* those foods that are *good for you*, the high-protein foods—those that are recommended by your doctor. But you will find it so easy and *effortless*, you will be proud of the fact that you can do this through the *power of your own mind*. You will be *pleased* and *proud* of your appearance. You will find the excess weight just *rolling off you*, just *melting away* from those parts of your body where there is too much. In a short time, you will be down to the weight that you want to be, to the size and the shape that you want to be. You can see yourself in your mind's eye exactly as you will be in a short time—*slim and shapely*, with exactly the size, the shape, the contours that you want to have."

The suggestions are couched in positive terms as much as possible. Such phrases as "You will find it easy," "You will get filling satisfaction from less food," "You will be proud of your appearance and your ability," help the subject to attain the proper frame of mind. The italicized words and phrases are the "key" elements in these suggestions.

The subject was also taught to hypnotize herself and to give herself suggestions while in a self-induced state. Such suggestions were prepared for her in advance because self-suggestions must be all the more carefully worded to make certain that they are positive suggestions.

In most cases, one or two sessions a week are sufficient. After the subject has been losing weight steadily for four or five weeks, the heterohypnotic sessions may be discontinued, but she must keep up the self-hypnotic reinforcement for a considerably longer time, until she has developed the proper eating habits.

BREAKING THE CIGARETTE HABIT

Case of C.B. The subject smoked two packs of cigarettes a day and felt it might prove injurious to his health. His doctor could not find anything physically wrong with him and recommended hypnosis.

C.B. was a medium depth subject, testing out for analgesia and amnesia after the third session. A system of cutting-down was used and after eight sessions he had completely given up the habit. After he was placed in hypnosis, suggestions were given as follows:

"For the coming week, you will smoke only a pack and a half a day. When you get up to-morrow morning, you will take two packs of cigarettes, empty one of them so that only ten cigarettes remain in it and make up your mind right then and there, *calmly but determinedly*, that those thirty cigarettes a day will be more than enough for you. You will indeed find thirty cigarettes a day *more than enough for you*. Somehow, your subconscious mind will apportion these thirty cigarettes over the day in such a way that you will not have any period of unusual deprivation. You will find thirty cigarettes a day *more than enough for you*. And don't be surprised, when you go to bed at night, if you have two or three cigarettes left over.

"Also, you will now be *aware* of your smoking. That is, from the time you reach for a cig-arette, light it and start to smoke, *you will be aware of what you 're doing every moment of the time*. Thus, since the main element of a habit is its unconscious or unaware aspect, we are simply tearing your smoking habit up by the roots. Since you are aware of what you are doing, you are no longer in the habit. However, I want you to continue smoking and to cut down gradually, in order to avoid an undue shock to your nervous system. This will make it *easy and effortless*. In fact, your awareness of your smoking may actually annoy you, so that you may wish to put the cigarette out while you are only half finished with it. It may not taste as good as it used to and you simply will not wish to continue."

The subject was also taught self-hypnosis, and the first week he was told to repeat, three times a day, the auto-suggestion: "I find 30 cigarettes a day more than enough for me." The second week he was cut down to a pack a day and continued the same procedure for the second week. When he came in for the third session he reported that he felt he did not want to cut down to ten cigarettes the next week, but only to fifteen, as he thought he might have some difficulty. His suggestion was accepted. Thereafter, he was cut down five cigarettes a day for each week. When he reached the point where he was only smoking five cigarettes a day, he felt that he could now stop completely. And he did.

The main elements in this system of breaking the cigarette habit are cutting down, creation of awareness, and self-hypnotic reinforcement. The awareness removes the unconscious compulsion to smoke and makes the cutting down process easy and effortless, because no conscious effort is needed. Deep hypnosis is not necessary for breaking the cigarette habit.

The old procedure of making cigarettes taste foul simply does not work well. Since post-hypnotic effects are temporary, and depend on trance depth, the subject quickly learns when the bad taste will wear off, he waits impatiently, and when the taste is normal again he goes back to smoking more heavily then ever and often makes up for lost time.

BREAKING THE NAIL-BITING HABIT

Case of Mrs. MA. This subject was actually referred by her doctor for diet control, but in the course of the initial interview she revealed that she would also like to stop the nail-biting habit, though she had little hope of succeeding. I phoned her doctor for permission to include this little project in my efforts and obtained it.

Five sessions, during which the subject entered a medium to deep trance, failed to produce any results with the diet control. A psychological evaluation to determine possible emotional reasons for this failure was not productive. After two more sessions the attempt to control the subject's diet was abandoned. However, in the process she completely stopped biting her nails—and after the very first lesson! Here was the procedure followed. While in hyp-nosis she was given these suggestions:

"Whenever you have the slightest desire to bite your nails—in fact, just as soon as you start raising your hand towards your mouth—you will instantly become *fully aware of what is going on*. You will therefore stop your hand about midway to your mouth and you will *pause and think* whether you actually do want to start biting your nails. You will be fully aware of your hand and you will stop to decide what you intend to do and what you really want to do. If you feel you really do want to bite your nails—well, then go right ahead and do it! But the chances are you will have no desire to do so—the chances are you *will prefer to lower your hand again*. That is, the mere *awareness of your hand will tend to dissipate* the compulsion to bite your nails—you are simply being given an awareness of the compulsion. As a result, the compulsion disappears; the energy behind the compulsion becomes completely dissipated—and you find that you do not really have any need to bite your nails."

This system works like a charm in many cases. Deep hypnosis is not required, but the deeper the hypnosis the more definite the awareness that is created. Often one session is sufficient, but it is always advisable to take a few more just to consolidate the gains made.

Case of J.L. Mindful of the fact that many experimenters in the field, especially psychiatrists, are constantly warning against symptom removal and the possibility of symptom-substitution (the possibility that removing one symptom will cause another and possibly a more harmful symptom to take its place), I now present such a case to illustrate that this eventuality can be easily detected and guarded against. However, this occurrence is extremely rare. In over thirty years, I have seen less than half a dozen cases in which nail-biting removal tended towards development of a substitute symptom; and in no case was the substitute symptom more serious than the original one. The psychologist with whom I am associated finds such reactions negligible on the basis of his own experience.

J.L. was the 11-year-old son of a dentist pupil of mine. In spite of a physician's referral and a psychologist's evaluation, I undertook the case with reluctance because I was aware that the boy's parents were having marital difficulties and that his nail-biting was probably a sign of his resulting feelings of insecurity; but there was a great deal of insistence on the part of the dentist and the physician that the attempt be made.

The boy was an instant somnambule, exhibiting all the classic signs of the somnambulic trance. He was given the "awareness" routine and told to return in a week. At the second session he came in with his mother rather than his father. His mother was very pleased, reporting that he had completely stopped biting his nails. Occasionally, she would find him "looking at his hands in a peculiar way," but he never actually raised them to his mouth. Incidentally, the mother did not know the technique that was used. The only thing that concerned her was that the boy, while watching television, would occasionally take his shoes off and pick on his toes.

He was rehypnotized and given awareness suggestions in connection with his toes, and sent home. At the third session, his mother reported that there was no nail-biting and no toe-picking—but now the boy had started making grimaces with his face!

At this juncture I pointed out very forcefully that the boy needed a deeper therapy and referred him to the psychologist. Actually, the possibility of symptom substitution showed up at the very second session and by the third session it was a sure thing. To continue removing symptoms when an emotional cause is apparent would be very foolish. It must also be pointed out that a lay hypnotist does not have the training and qualifications to enable him to search for these hidden causes; this comes properly within the work of psychiatrists and clinical psychologists.

HYPNOTIC CONDITIONING FOR CHILDBIRTH

Case of Mrs. HG. The expectant mother was placed in hypnosis and taught how to hypnotize herself by taking a deep breath and counting back from five to one as she exhaled. Then she was instructed to count back mentally from fifty to one while she was in the self-induced hypnotic state; then she was to awaken herself by counting forward from one to five. She was instructed to perform this exercise three times daily in order to condition herself.

It was explained to her that the procedure of counting back from fifty had the effect of producing anesthesia in those parts of the body which were involved in the processes of labor and delivery. When she was ready to go to the hospital, she was to hypnotize herself just before she felt a contraction coming on and then count backward from fifty during the contractions. The act of counting was a post-hypnotic suggestion which would make her anesthetic so that she could feel none of the pain of the contractions—only the pressure and the movements. When the contraction was over she was to awaken herself by counting from one to five. She was to keep this up until she was taken to the delivery room, at which point the obstetrician would take over. In response to a post-hypnotic signal, she would again go into hypnosis when the doctor uttered the words "Close your eyes, relax and sleep!" Thereafter the doctor would proceed in the usual way, but would simply make suggestions of anesthesia instead of using chemical agents.

At least the third stage of hypnosis is needed for anesthesia during childbirth, but often, for normal deliveries, even lighter stages of relaxation are helpful in eliminating apprehension and in dulling the pains of childbirth. For episiotomys and for other surgical procedures, at least a fourth stage is required, and sometimes chemical anesthetics are used in conjunction.

The hypno-technician does not appear in the hospital; all his work is done beforehand. The physician, naturally, needs a briefing if he has no previous experience with hypnosis. Also, it is advisable for the technician and the obstetrician to get together with the patient at least once in order for the hypnotist to transfer *rapport* to the doctor. Hypnotic conditioning for childbirth may be effectively done in groups.

HYPNOTIC CONDITIONING FOR DENTISTRY

Case of L.O.R. The patient was referred by a dentist who had no experience with hypnosis and wanted to perform the extraction of a second lower molar entirely via post-hypnotic suggestion. Usually, it is preferable that the technician goes to the dentist's office to act as "anesthetist" but the distance made this procedure prohibitive.

In three sessions the patient was conditioned into the fourth stage. He was then taught to hypnotize himself, to produce anesthesia in his right hand and to transfer the anesthesia to his lower jaw by rubbing it with his hand. Then, to maintain the anesthesia during the operation, he was told to keep a moving contact of his hands on the arms of the chair and to keep his mind on this contact.

When the subject finally went to the dentist's office, he was fully confident of his ability to carry on by himself. The operation was a rather difficult one, lasting nearly half an hour, but the subject, without any help whatever from the dentist, was able to remain in hypnosis and to keep the anesthetic state active in the manner described above.

It must be stressed that, under painful stimulation, anesthesia wears off rapidly; hence the necessity for "doing something" self-hypnotically to maintain the anesthesia. Naturally, when the operator is present, his suggestions serve the purpose. Of course, *rapport* can be transferred to the dentist, whose suggestions would then keep the anesthesia in effect.

HYPNOTIC CONDITIONING FOR SURGERY

Case of E. T. A fourteen-year-old girl, E.T. had a heart condition, which made the use of chemical anesthesia dangerous in a knee operation for the removal of a displaced ligament. She went into a light fifth stage (light somnambulism) and was conditioned to respond to suggestions on a tape recorder, which was brought into the operating room. Actually, she was able to hypnotize herself easily, but she was not able to remain in hypnosis for long without my presence; I would not be admitted to the operating room because I am not a physician, and the surgeon did not feel competent to take over the rapport of the subject, having no previous experience with hypnosis. The suggestions on the tape are reproduced below in some-what condensed form:

"Evelyn, as I count from one to five, you go easily and deeply into a hypnotic state. One—two—three—four—five ... go deep asleep now! Go way down into a very deep, sound and restful hypnotic sleep! That's fine. Deep asleep.

"Now you know, of course, that you are about to have your knee fixed up. You have every confidence in your doctor and I have assured you that you will feel no pain or discomfort of any sort. As I am talking to you, the operation begins, but you are completely unconcerned about what is going on. You know your left leg is there and that they are working on it, but you have a strange feeling that the leg does not belong to you, that it belongs to someone else temporarily, until the operation is over and it is fixed up properly.

"Now take your mind fully off your leg and think of what I am saying. My words seem to fill your mind, fill your awareness, so that you cannot really think of anything else. In fact, I will now start to count backward from 100. Each count will seem to push you deeper and deeper into hypnosis. Each count makes you less and less aware of your leg, because your leg is completely anesthetic, you see, and you could not feel anything in it even if you tried. Each count makes your leg more and more anesthetic, and pushes you deeper and deeper into hypnosis at the same time. Now, as I count, I want you to anticipate the next count. That is, as I say 100, you think ahead to 99—as I say 99, you think of 98—as I say 98, you think of 97—and so on. In other words, you will be busy listening to me and thinking ahead to the next number at the same time. This will occupy your mind so fully that you will not be able to think of your leg or of anything else."

Then there was counting from one hundred down to eighty. For a few moments suggestions were given about her leg "being completely insensible to pain" and that her mind remained fully occupied with the counting. Then the counting continued for a while longer, followed by additional suggestions of anesthesia. The important thing for the student to remember is that anesthesia, under painful stimulation, depends upon the subject's mind being engrossed with things that simply distract from the operation itself. For this purpose, a running commentary of suggestions is necessary. If no suggestions are given, the anesthesia would be likely to "wear off" rather rapidly.

In the Case of E.T., when the operation was over the doctor awakened her upon a post-hypnotic signal and she was taken back to her room. The anesthesia in her leg, however, remained in accordance with suitable suggestions on the tape. Two hours later I came in to see her. The anesthesia was just beginning to wear off, so she was hypnotized again with suggestions that her leg would remain anesthetic through the night and that in the morning, although the feeling would be back, there would be no pain because the healing process was already well under way. Suggestions for rapid healing were also made.

HYPNOSIS IN BREAKING URINARY RETENTION

Case of Mrs. F. C. S. This is a remarkable case in which a single hypnotic session corrected a condition on which medical science had given up.

I received an emergency call from Beth Israel Hospital of Newark, New Jersey at 11:00 clock on St. Patrick's Day morning. The patient, a woman of 51, had undergone a plastic repair of a cystocele and rectocele 13 days previously. After the operation, she was unable to urinate, a not uncommon condition following this type of surgery. To make matters worse, this condition persisted unduly long, which necessitated frequent catheterization. To avoid undue catheterization, the patient was given salt solutions to drink and all the drugs and tranquilizers that the doctors could think of were administered. But all to no avail.

When hypnosis was proposed as a last resort, the surgeon on the case laughed, saying that hypnosis could not possibly do any good after all the drugs had failed. Finally, however, the attending physician had me called in.

Mrs. E.C.S. was a beautiful Irish woman with a red rose in her hair. She greeted me with the remark that I was her last hope of spending this St. Patrick's Day at home with her family. If I could not help her, she said, then she could see nothing ahead but Overbrook (a medical institution).

In questioning Mrs. E.C.S., I found that she had been catheterized that morning. This was an adverse circumstance; had her bladder been full, hypnotic suggestion could have had an immediate effect, but under the circumstances the desired effects would have to come from post-hypnotic suggestion. Another very important consideration was, of course, that her muscle tone was probably impaired due to the almost daily catheterization. The outlook was not promising at all, but I naturally assumed a very confident air and assured the patient that hypnosis would do the trick.

I knew, moreover, that whatever was done must be accomplished in one session, as I certainly would not have the opportunity of a second attempt. It was therefore important that everything that was said or done be calculated to produce the desired effect.

No preliminary tests were performed, to avoid the letdown effect of possible failure. Mrs. E.C.S. was seated in a comfortable chair and, while the nurse guarded the door against possible visitors, I proceeded with the relaxation method of induction. Twenty-five minutes were spent in this procedure.

The patient appeared relaxed, but the only observable symptoms of hypnosis were the absence of voluntary movements and a slight drooping of the head. No challenges were attempted. The hypnosis, if it were indeed hypnosis, was so superficial that any slight failure would have stopped everything short.

I then proceeded to give her strong suggestions for the resumption of normal functioning. I explained that hypnosis had a definite post-hypnotic effect, so that when her bladder filled up again she would easily and effortlessly proceed to void. I gave her instructions that when she went to the lavatory, she would start counting backward from 100 in order to keep her mind off the process; I explained, too, that this counting procedure was in effect a post-hypnotic suggestion in response to which the subconscious mind would proceed to restore normal functioning. After fifteen minutes of strong suggestion, Mrs. E.C.S. was awakened.

Her first reaction was to question the fact that this was hypnosis. She was reassured on this score in a firm and confident way, but I realized that the patient was by no means convinced. I waited for the opportunity to play my ace card; the opportunity came with her question as to what the fee was.

I told her what my fee was and added: "But ... you don't pay me until *after* you see that my work has accomplished the intended purpose. Send me a check in the morning—from home."

And then, as I picked up my hat and started to leave, I said:

"YOU WILL HAVE A HAPPY ST. PATRICK'S DAY! Good-bye!"

Mrs. E.C.S. did not obey all the above "post-hypnotic" suggestions to the letter. I *received* the check the very next day—she *sent it* from the hospital less than half an hour after I left, and immediately after she emptied her bladder for the first time in 13 days without the aid of a catheter. She was discharged from the hospital that afternoon after voiding spontaneously several times. Accompanying the check was the following note:

"I certainly am most grateful for your help and your name will be one that I'll remember for a long time."

This is an excellent illustration of the effectiveness of light hypnotic or hypnoidal suggestion combined with skillfully applied indirect suggestion.

ENURESIS (Bed-Wetting)

Case of F.G. This is a spectacular illustration of the results achieved in a case of enuresis through a single application of hypnotic suggestion. It must be stressed that this is an unusual case, the success of which was due largely to the circumstances surrounding the first and only hypnotic session. In most cases of enuresis, the therapy is more time consuming and should be applied in a medical or psychiatric setting.

The subject was a 10-year-old boy. Presenting on the surface a picture of a lively, intelligent, vibrantly healthy child, he was self-conscious and unhappy about his inability to stop wetting his bed. He and his mother were taking therapy at a child guidance clinic to discover and erase any underlying emotional causes. The psychologist admitted frankly that it might be quite some time before the troublesome habit itself would be corrected. When asked if he had any objection to the use of hypnosis for removing the symptom, he replied in the negative, but warned that attendance at the clinic must not be interrupted.

The fortunate circumstance in this case was that T.G. was a friend and playmate of my son. The prestige factor was very strong; nevertheless T.G. was reluctant to confide in me because of his fear that his friend would learn of his habit. This difficulty was circumvented by arranging a social meeting between our two families, during which I was prevailed upon (!) to perform some group experiments using my wife and son and T.G. as subjects. The boy was found to be an excellent subject. Care was taken that he would remember everything upon awakening from the mass hypnosis, to eliminate any possibility of distrust. However, in the course of the experiments several post-hypnotic suggestions were unobtrusively introduced to the effect that after awakening T.G. would be most anxious to be hypnotized alone and in private. Everything was done in a light vein; T.G. 's difficulty was not mentioned at any time.

After the group was awakened, T.G. did an admirable job of maneuvering me away from the group and into a bedroom, where he fell into deep hypnosis very quickly. I immediately dropped all pretenses, declaring very authoritatively that T. G. 's bed-wetting was now a thing of the past. A veritable barrage of suggestions followed, to the effect that T.G. would never again wet the bed and would be a happier and more contented boy as a consequence. I spoke in terms of the pride the boy would have in his dry bed every morning—that he no longer would be different from other boys he knew. He now could participate in the overnight hikes of his scout troop with perfect safety. Upon awakening every morning, he would run to his mother and tell her with great pride that his bed was dry. Feelings of increasing confidence and well-being were instilled repeatedly. No questions or doubts were entertained in these suggestions; every vestige of prestige that I had in T.G.'s eyes was allowed to have its full effect. I also recounted (and invented) other cases of enuresis that I had "cured" in one sitting. The entire attitude was one of assumption that T.G. 's trouble was over and done with once and for all time. No amnesia was suggested, but T.G. was told that his mother (and only she) would be taken into our confidence.

The boy's mother played an important part in the actual therapy. She was instructed, at bedtime that evening, to remove the rubber sheet from T.G.'s bed very ostentatiously and happily, with simultaneous remarks to the effect that this nuisance was no longer needed and that she was discarding it forever. She was further instructed in the administration of indirect suggestion at every opportunity, and warned never for a moment to suggest or otherwise entertain doubts of the outcome.

No efforts were made to restrict his fluids at bedtime, as had previously been attempted without avail. He had been told under hypnosis, however, that he would awaken as soon as his bladder filled up sufficiently and immediately go to the bathroom. His mother was to remind him gently of this every night as a means of recharging the original suggestion; the reminder, having been suggested under hypnosis, was in itself a post-hypnotic suggestion.

Though the procedure on the surface was a comparatively simple one, the experienced hypnotists should recognize the important ingredients that contributed to the successful outcome—the prestige of the operator, the indirect, delicate handling at the start, the excellence of a subject of this age and the intelligent cooperation of the mother. The fact that they were being handled at the Child Guidance Clinic at the same time may have had an important bearing on the case. It should also be pointed out that the removal of the troublesome symptom may, by the same token, have had a bearing on the successful completion of the work at the clinic.

LESSON SEVENTEEN
PRACTICAL USES OF HYPNOSIS
(Continued)

NON-THERAPEUTIC APPLICATIONS
Because the non-therapeutic applications are considered educational tools rather than medical techniques, a physician's referral may not be required. However, because a lay hypnotist is not qualified to make a diagnosis, in cases of doubt a medical referral should be resorted to as a precautionary measure. The cases that follow are samplings of non-therapeutic applications of hypnosis:

FACILITATING THE LEARNING PROCESS
Case of G.M. The subject was a 37-year-old law student who had already failed the bar exam twice. He simply could not afford to fail a third time and wanted to use all the necessary means to assure his success. Naturally, because of his age, his learning ability was not as good as it had been when he was younger. He was sent to a psychologist to evaluate his chances and to ascertain that there were no serious emotional problems that might serve as stumbling blocks in the way of success in this project. No contraindications were found.

G.M. never attained anything beyond a hypnoidal state; nevertheless he was taught the techniques of self-hypnosis and was given a series of suggestions to use during his self-hypnotic exercises. These suggestions, as well as those given heterohypnotically, were slanted to cope with the three major factors in learning—impression, retention and recall. Suggestions to increase *impression* were couched in the following terms:

"When you sit down to study, you will find yourself *completely absorbed and fully engrossed in what you are doing.* Outside sounds will not bother you. Things that used to distract you in the past will seem to *roll off you like water rolls off a duck's back.* You will be completely *unconcerned with everything around you* as you study; you will be fully engrossed in your material to the exclusion of all else. Thus, concentration is assured. Since you will be concentrating spontaneously—without any effort—the material you are studying will make *deep and lasting impressions* in your mind. Everything you read will make *deep and indelible impressions* on your subconscious. As a result of these deep impressions, your retention of all the *material you learn will be lasting and permanent.*" The italicized suggestions are the key suggestions for the purpose of increasing impression and assuring *retention.* To facilitate the recall factor, the following suggestions were made:

"Whatever you have learned will be *easily and readily recalled* whenever you need it. When taking examinations, you will find facts and figures and other needed material flowing freely and easily through your mind. There will be rio grope and strain for material that you have learned but have forgotten, as in the past. Now, because your subconscious mind is working for you, things come much more quickly and certainly much more easily. There is no effort involved at all. Whatever you have learned is released by your subconscious, which is a giant storehouse, whenever you need it. Therefore, whatever you have earned flows freely and easily though your mind, without any effort on your part. The fact that you are relaxed Facilitates this process greatly."

79

The subject was also taught a more methodical study technique, in which he studied for briefer periods with short periods of rest in between. He was also advised to hypnotize himself occasionally during the rest periods in order to eliminate fatigue and promote concentration. All the studying is done in the waking state, with post-hypnotic suggestion providing the benefits. Studying under hypnosis is not an effective method unless the material to be learned is to be committed to memory by rote. Rote memorizing does not assure the integration of the material into the individual's previous fund of knowledge.

G.M. reported marked improvement in concentration and recall after three sessions. After eight sessions the training was terminated. Two months later he took his bar exam, and passed.

IMPROVING SALES ABILITY

Case of R.H. R.H. was an insurance salesman who suffered from some of the common faults found in this profession: lack of self-confidence, poor planning, lack of drive, low rate of "cold calls," and the tendency to ego-deflation whenever a door was slammed in his face. He was taught self-hypnosis and, through ten sessions, one fault at a time was tackled and eliminated or minimized.

Planning was the first item corrected. The suggestions given, both heterohypnotically and self-hypnotically, were centered around the key suggestion, *"Plan your work and work your plan."* Of course, the subject was urged to sit down several times a week and plan his work for the next few days consciously. The suggestions simply reinforced his desire to "carry out his plan." Next his "drive" was increased, as a result of which he was easily able to make a prescribed number of "cold calls" each day.

His tendency towards ego-deflation and his lack of confidence were connected and took considerably longer to correct. In regard to his lack of self-confidence, he spent two sessions with a psychologist to give him some working insight into his problems. Thereafter it was reasonably easy for him to develop a kind of "immunity" to slamming doors; the key suggestion centered around the idea of the irritations and the annoyances of everyday life "rolling off him like water rolls off a duck's back." Picturesque expressions like the above seem to more readily penetrate into the subconscious.

In general, a subject's individual faults must be analyzed and specific suggestions formulated to cope with those faults. Those suggestions are then administered heterohypnotically and self-hypnotically; the hypnotic suggestions of the operator make deeper impressions on the subconscious initially, and the subject's auto-suggestions serve to reinforce or "recharge" the hetero-affirmations.

In a manner of speaking, hypnosis for salesmen is similar to the "pep talks" they receive from the sales managers regularly. But whereas the "pep talks" wear off rapidly due to the fact that their effect is superficial, hypnosis, reinforced with self-hypnosis, has a constantly self-reactivating effect.

HYPNOSIS FOR REMEDIAL READING

Case of Dr. F. V. Dr. F.V. was an engineer with an important supervisory position. He was required to do a lot of technical reading in order to keep up with advances in his field. He had always been a rather slow reader, but he was now really beginning to feel the effects of this deficiency.

Five sessions failed to increase his reading speed appreciably, in spite of the fact that he was a good medium-depth subject. However, there was a marked change in the gross result of his reading; he was now getting much more out of it. His comprehension of the material was much greater, and he was now able to find the technical material more meaningful and therefore easier to assimilate.

This is a good example of a case where a subject thinks his faults lie in one area, whereas the actual trouble is elsewhere.

HYPNOSIS IN SPORTS

Case of J.M. The subject was a professional bowler. He was able to get good scores but was troubled with the fact that his performance was so inconsistent. Upon questioning it was found that when J.M. felt "good" he did very well in a game, but on those occasions when "doubts crept into his mind" he could drop down as much as thirty points.

The work commenced with suggestions to the effect that when he bowled he would be, "completely unconcerned with everything around him except what he was doing," on the theory that distractions throw one off. Suggestions of being "absorbed in his throw" were also given for the same purpose, and suggestions of general self-confidence and self-assurance were added. His game improved slightly. Then this formula was attempted:

"When you are about to step forward for your throw, stop for a moment, close your eyes, and see in your mind's eye the exact spot where you want your ball to hit—where it is going to hit. Then open your eyes and aim for the spot that you visualized."

It must be stressed that no one formula will be equally effective for everyone. It is an individual matter. An attempt must be made to find just where the subject is having trouble, and suggestions must be formulated to cope with the situation that exists. When one suggestion does not work, others should be tried until the right formula is found.

In the case of J.M., the suggestion to visualize a strike just before stepping up for the throw caused his mind to become "set" on that idea, thereby preventing the last-moment doubt that usually "threw him off."

HYPNOSIS IN LAW-ENFORCEMENT

Law-enforcement is actually a fertile field for the applications of hypnosis, but the old stigmas and misconceptions are so strong among the authorities that law-enforcement officers generally are very cautious in their espousal of this science. Generally speaking, hypnosis may be applied in these areas:

1. Amnesia-breaking
2. Interrogation
3. Lie-detection (with or without the polygraph)
4. Facilitating recall

The following brief case studies should give the reader a rough idea of how hypnosis is and has been employed in these areas:

BREAKING AN AMNESIA CASE

Case of J.R. Sheriff "Dave" Star of Orange County, Florida called in Joe McCawley, my star pupil and good friend, to examine a man who was picked up in a dazed condition, with complete amnesia for events prior to that day. Sheriff Star had become familiar with the possibilities of hypnosis only the previous week, when I appeared on the same TV program with him and later was invited to address his detectives on the subject.

In three sessions, the technician was able to clear up the man's memory completely and send him on his way.

Case of D. C. The subject, a 12-year-old boy, witnessed a hold-up—at least, that part of it where the hold-up man dashed out of a hardware store, got into a car, and drove off. He was able to describe the man and the car but could only remember the first two digits in the license number. On questioning, by a detective, the boy became confused, so that eventually, instead of remembering more of the number, he was no longer certain of the first two digits. I was then called in by county detectives.

The boy proved to be a somnambule. During questioning under hypnosis he was able to recall many details of the car and the hold-up man that he had not previously told. Mindful of the confusion in the boy's mind regarding the license number, this matter was not even touched upon at the beginning. Finally, the following suggestions were made:

The full story of this amazing case appears in Vol. V No. 1 of *Hypnosis Quarterly*.

"Now, I want you to see a blackboard in front of you. tell me when you see it clearly. Fine! Now if you look closely, you will notice that the blackboard is covered with a piece of velvet cloth—dark velvet cloth. Do you see it? Fine! Now, there is something beneath that cloth that you naturally cannot see. That is, you cannot see it now because it is covered. But in a moment, I shall whisk that cloth aside and you will see very clearly what is beneath that cloth on the blackboard. Don't even be concerned about what it is; you don't need to be, because you will soon see it very clearly, right before your eyes. When I whisk the cloth away, you will see a license plate there hung on the blackboard—the license plate that was on the car in that hold-up. Right now you see nothing but the velvet cloth, but in a moment, as I count "Three! And whisk the cloth away, you will see that license plate very clearly and you will call out the number instantly. Call it out instantly— without thinking. Now ... one-two—three! There goes the cloth! You see the number! Now, tell us—what is the number you see?"

The boy rattled off a number without the slightest hesitation. The number was checked and found to be that of a car belonging to a man in another city. The car had been stolen from a parking lot, used in the hold-up and returned to the lot.

The tricky part of this case was the necessity of clearing the boy's mind of the confusion caused by his trying to recall the number consciously. It is a well-known fact that conscious efforts to remember often have the opposite to the desired effect. It is not likely that the hallucination ruse would have worked on a lighter subject. Age regression is another technique that could have been used in this case.

Case of J. C. The subject was being held on $20,000 bail as a material witness in a murder case. His girl friend had confessed to killing a man who, she claimed, tried to make advances to her. But she implicated her boy friend, who, she said, helped her dispose of the body. J.C., however, disclaimed any knowledge of the matter, protesting that at the time he was at work running an elevator in a mine.

When ordinary interrogation failed, the man was subjected to a polygraph (lie-detection) examination. However, he was so nervous during the examination that the findings were not considered valid. I was called in at this point.

J.C. was a light subject. He could not be pushed beyond the third stage at the most. However, he was so relaxed that a polygraph examination, conducted post-hypnotically with the suggestion that he would remain relaxed, came out so well that the examiners were able to state conclusively that he was telling the truth.

Moreover, during another hypnotic induction immediately following the polygraph examination, a "rapid-fire" interrogation technique was used which further substantiated the findings that he was innocent. In this technique, he was told to respond to simple questions instantly, without stopping to think. He did so with split-second precision, even responding to "test" questions like, "Do you masturbate?" without a moment's pause. J.C. 's bail was reduced to $5,000 and shortly after he was completely exonerated.

Case of Mrs. F.L.P. The subject accused a physician of making improper advances to her while she was under hypnosis and threatened to take him to court. The doctor, however, had tape-recorded all sessions with this patient without her knowledge; his attorney consulted with the woman's lawyer and all concerned agreed to subject her to a hypnotic lie-detection examination. I was called in to perform the examination with the "automatic response" technique, which I had a hand in originating.

The woman was a medium-to-deep subject. Under hypnosis, she was conditioned to develop an uncontrollable twitch of her right forefinger whenever her wrist was touched. When this worked repeatedly, she was then told that the same twitch would occur at the count of "three." Both touch and count of "three" were given repeatedly until the twitch of her forefinger was absolutely uncontrollable. She was even unable to resist the twitch when told to try as hard as possible. Then she received the following suggestion:

"When you are awake, every time you lie your finger will twitch just as it does when I touch your wrist, or when I count to three. You will be completely unable to control this twitch: in fact, the harder you try to control it, the more violently your finger will jump."

Then she was awakened and the lawyers asked her the pertinent questions. She continued to lie like a trooper—but her telltale forefinger gave her away unmistakably! This method is well nigh foolproof with subjects who are responsive to ideo-motor responses. Naturally, the purpose of the twitch should not be revealed to the subject until the response is quite out of his control. This method works better when the subject has post-hypnotic amnesia, but even when he is fully aware of what is going on and tries hard to control himself, the autonomic response comes through.

HYPNOSIS FOR STAGE FRIGHT

Case of Mrs. F.L. The subject was a 40-year-old woman who had been an operatic singer prior to her marriage eighteen years ago. Now, with two teen-age children who no longer required daily care, she wanted to resume her interrupted career; in fact, she was well on the way to a comeback and was scheduled to sing at the Metropolitan Opera House in New York in two weeks. She came to me because, having been away from the limelight for so long, she feared she might "freeze up" before a vast audience. Having had a history of stage fright in her early years, she naturally feared a recurrence. A psychological check up found her to be in good emotional shape.

Since she only had two weeks for the training, a series of three sessions was agreed upon. She was taught self-hypnosis, and she was instructed to give herself suggestions to the effect that her first appearance on the stage would be "so exhilarating and successful," that she would "look forward to her new success with pleasurable anticipation," that she was "resuming her career with perfect self-assurance and self-confidence" and that "the sight of a large and appreciative audience would fill her with warm pleasure and unbounded self-confidence."

The reader will notice that such words as "fear," "freezing up," "stage fright" and similar negative expressions were completely absent from the self-hypnotic suggestions. As a result of this training, Mrs. F.L. became so imbued with "pleasurable anticipation" that she, in effect, "forgot" to be afraid of the coming event.

Case of P. W. The 30-year-old subject was a member of a local drama group. He had been doing quite well in small supporting parts, but now he was to star in a play, which required memorizing a long script. Time was running out and he was far behind schedule in mastering the script. Moreover, because of the importance of doing well in his first starring role, his anxiety was so great that he had build up a lot of tension, which further hindered his work. He turned to hypnosis in desperation.

P.W. was a very poor subject; in fact, he failed to enter even the first stage of hypnosis. However, he was taught Dr. Hornell Hart's variety of auto-conditioning and kept up his exercises religiously.*

In seven sessions he lost most of his tension and was well on the way to mastering the script. In addition to suggestions of relaxation, he was also given suggestions of confidence, expectation of success, and was taught a study method in which he studied for 15-minute periods, which were broken up with ten-minute rest periods devoted to listening to hi-fi music. He did very well on opening night and had no problems thereafter.

*Dr. Hart's method relies largely on "progressive relaxation" with suggestions being given regardless of the presence of absence of hypnosis.

ADDENDA

THE THREE STEPS IN THE
SELF-HYPNOSIS
TRAINING PROCEDURE

These are the three basic steps that I now employ almost invariably in training subjects for self-hypnosis. Variations in induction technique and method of testing for the existence of hypnosis may occur. Also, in the third step, the actual formula (auto-suggestion) used varies with the subject's purpose.

Step 1.
Hypnosis is induced via Progressive Relaxation or any similar method. No bizarre method is employed. Actually, the subject is not promised anything insofar as the production-tion of an actual hypnotic trance is concerned. He is merely placed in a receptive "subjective" state of mind (in the sense that the hypnotic state is a "subjective" condition, he is in hypnosis). He is then instructed somewhat as follows:
"In this condition, your subconscious mind is at the forefront; it is now readily accessible to my suggestions to you. Therefore, I shall now teach you the first exercise in your self-hypnosis (or auto-conditioning) training.
"When you go to bed at night—starting tonight—you will get into your favorite position for sleep and make yourself nice and comfortable. Then you will repeat 20 times the auto-suggestion formula *Positive thinking brings me the advantages that I desire.* You will repeat this to yourself, but it will help if you move your lips to form the words—if you mouth the words. To keep count, you will use the fingers of both hands. You will press down slightly with the little finger of your right hand—and say the suggestion once. Then you will press down with the ring finger and say it a second time. Then you will use the middle finger, the forefinger and the thumb, repeating the suggestion with each finger. You will do the same with the left hand, making it ten times, again with the right, making it fifteen, and again with the left, thus completing twenty repetitions.
"You will do this every night for seven nights. You must not allow yourself to fall asleep until the twenty repetitions have been completed. This is necessary in order to establish a conditioned reflex, a sort of habit pattern, which is produced by the combination of a thought in your mind with the physical movement of your fingers. Thus, in seven nights a kind of channel of communication is established between your conscious and subconscious minds through this conditioned reflex. This reflex, gradually coinciding with your "twilight state" (which closely resembles the hypnotic state) assures that the suggestion gets into your subconscious as you fall asleep."

Step 2.
Rehypnotized via any method, the subject is again instructed as follows:
"You will continue doing the exercise you learned last week, but you need not stay awake

for twenty repetitions now if you feel like falling asleep sooner. Thus, as you fall asleep, the suggestion in your mind at the time simply drops into your subconscious. Then, while you are peacefully sleeping, it does its work in the subconscious sphere, producing the results that you are seeking without any effort on your part. But now I shall teach you how to place yourself in a subjective (or hypnotic or auto-conditioned) state.

"Three times a day—once in the morning, once at noon or early afternoon and once in the evening—you will hypnotize yourself, stay in hypnosis for about three minutes, and then awaken yourself Here's how you will do this:

"You will sit down or lie down, place your attention on some spot on the wall opposite you—or on the ceiling if you are lying down—and take five deep breaths. As you inhale the fifth breath, you will do so extra deeply and you will hold your breath for about five seconds. As you hold the fifth breath, you will count down, mentally, from five to one, exhale as you do so, close your eyes, and sink into a deep, relaxing subjective (hypnotic) state. Actually, this is a post-hypnotic suggestion, which will enable you to drop into hypnosis as you count from five to one.

"You will remain in hypnosis for about three minutes. To maintain the hypnotic level, you will now count down, mentally, from 50 to 1. You will do this easily—semi-automatically, as this too is a post-hypnotic suggestion. The procedure of counting will keep you in a hypnotic state, whereas if you did nothing the state would rapidly dissipate. Then, to awaken, you will simply count forward from one to five-and this will awaken you, as this too is a post-hypnotic suggestion.

"You will do this three times a day for seven days. This too will become a conditioned reflex—an easy, semi-automatic process. Then you will be ready to start giving yourself appropriate suggestions." And you awaken the subject. It is advisable to rehearse him with the procedure immediately, while it is fresh in his mind, to make certain that he understands it perfectly. This rehearsing also tends to produce a good "set."

Step 3.
At the third session a week later, you place the subject in hypnosis again (or you allow him to hypnotize himself via the method he has learned) and give him the following instructions:

"After I awaken you, I shall help you prepare a suitable suggestion that you will now start to use. If it is your desire to learn how to attain a relaxed state, our suggestion might be worded like this: *I am completely relaxed at all times, both mentally and physically.* Whatever your needs are, we will develop an appropriate suggestion. This suggestion will be written on a card, and you will use it in this manner:

"Just before you hypnotize yourself three times a day, you will go through the procedure of reading the card five times. That is, you will get yourself in the proper position for hypnosis, pick a spot on the wall in readiness, hold the card up before you in one hand, and read it over, mentally, five times, concentrating hard on the words as you do so. Immediately after the fifth reading, you will drop your hand holding the card and simultaneously look up at the spot on the wall and take your first breath. Then the second, third, fourth and fifth breaths. On the fifth breath you will count back from five to one as you hold it, exhale, and drop into Hypnosis. As you go into hypnosis the words in your conscious mind automatically slip into your subconscious.

"Now you do nothing except lie passively. You need not count any more, because the counting has already served its purpose. But you will now find, as you lie or sit there passively, that the words on the card are now in your mind—in your subconscious mind—going around in a peculiar, semi-automatic way. You will find the words mulling around in your mind, reverberating in a strange way—going around and around and around in your mind by themselves, without any conscious effort on your part. We might say that this is effortless, spontaneous, subconscious thinking—in which the conscious mind has no real part.

"All at once you will feel that the time is up—that is, the time that you conditioned yourself to remain in hypnosis by counting back from fifty. You may feel like the words are slowing up or stopping, or your eyes may pop open, or it may seem like a light has gone on in the room. Or, you may simply have a vague feeling that the time is up. Whereupon you will immediately count from one to five and awaken.

"You need not be concerned about the time. Leave it all to your subconscious. Your subconscious will awaken you when your time is up, that time having become set by your counting back from 50 to 1." The time will vary with individuals, of course, depending upon the speed with which they counted.

Then you awaken the subject, prepare a card for him, preferably something that will serve a useful purpose, and watch him perform the experiment as you had instructed him (without giving him any pre-warning of this) and note how long he remains in hypnosis.

"The accuracy of his 'time-set' will serve as an indication of his being in hypnosis. Also, if he reports the semi-automatic quality of his subconscious thinking, this too will serve not only as an indication to you but as a convincing item for him. Thus the need for testing for hypnosis via 'challenges,' which often fail, is obviated. Of course, should there be sufficient subjective indications of the presence of hypnosis (feelings of floating, numbness, tingling, detachment, etc.) tests in the form of 'challenges' will be additionally convincing to the subject."

The subject then practices this method of pre-hypnotic suggestion three times daily for a week. Usually, some results show up at once—and this is the real "convincer" for anyone.

The importance of the proper formulation of auto-suggestion cannot be stressed too strongly; suggestions must always be couched in positive terms.

Regarding the contents of this book.

In the late 40s and early 50s, outside the mainstream psychology world, most of the so-called books that were published about hypnotism would be considered folios or booklets and would often be mimeographed, since xeroxing (photocopying) wasn't yet on the scene. In our Hypno-Classics™ series we have brought many of these long out-of-print booklets together in compilation for those in the 21st century who are students of the art and science of hypnotism—the avid hypnologist.

Our new publication, *The Best of Harry Arons, The Master Course in Hypnotism, Power Hypnosis, and The Best of Rexford L. North* and the Boston Hypnotism Center present information from the past that is still applicable to present day hypnotism practices. Now we are bringing these classics as they were originally written to you in a reasonably-priced, contemporary format. Whether you have purchased this book for its historical value in your library or with the hope of learning something new we thank you for your interest in what is an important part of the development of hypnotism in America after WWII.

Order these today at
ngh@ngh.net
www.ngh.net

Harry Arons

About the writer:

Harry Arons died of heart failure, September 9, 1997. He had a long and distinguished career in the field of hypnotism. In the early thirties he performed as a stage hypnotist throughout the New Jersey/New York area and spent several seasons entertaining at Atlantic City and Asbury Par as well as on the summer resort hotel circuit.

In the forties there was a good market in mail-order and with the title of Power Publishers, Arons built a large client list for his Master Course in Hypnotism and other titles through advertising in the popular pulp magazines of the time. His base of operations was South Orange, New Jersey, an area where he had lived since coming to this country with his family as a teenager. He told friends that his native Lithuania he had learned about hypnotism from his grandfather, who was allegedly a friend of the famed Rasputin.

At this time he also conducted regular classes for those who wanted personal instruction in mastering the mysteries of hypnosis. These classes led to his beginning, as owner/director, of the Ethical Hypnosis Training Center in New Jersey. This teaching facility provided a base for further expansion as he took his courses to various cities throughout the United States.

A prolific writer, Arons was an associate editor of the fledgling Journal of Hypnotism and contributed many popular articles such as; *How*

To Make Money With Hypnotism, Hypnotic Conditioning for Childbirth, Instantaneous Hypnosis, How To Hypnotize Yourself. This affiliation continued from May 1951 through February 1953, when his energies were turned to a new organization which was being formed.

With a group of twenty or so health professionals, most of whom had been his hypnosis students, Arons formed the Association for the Advancement of Ethical Hypnosis in 1954. The group consisted of physicians, psychologists, dentists, lawyers, ministers, etc., but also later admitted qualified lay hypnotists, who were called "hypno-technicians," and who were allowed to use hypnosis for therapeutic purposes only under medical supervision.

With the advent and subsequent growth of the AAEH, Arons also served as editor of Hypnosis magazine and Hypnosis Quarterly as he continued teaching and writing. In 1959, Arons widened his teaching to law enforcement personnel and in 1967 his textbook, Hypnosis in Criminal Investigation, was published. He is generally credited with being the first hypnotist to formally write about and teach what we know as forensic hypnosis.

Breinigsville, PA USA
22 November 2010
249802BV00001B/6/P